THE HISTORY OF NBA BASKETBALL
THAT NOBODY TALKS ABOUT
FOR KIDS

*With Unbelievable
Inspiring Stories & Forgotten Stats*

WILLIAM LAWSON

© **Copyright 2022 - All rights reserved.**
The content contained within this book may not be reproduced, duplicated or transmitted without direct written permission from the author or the publisher.

Under no circumstances will any blame or legal responsibility be held against the publisher, or author, for any damages, reparation, or monetary loss due to the information contained within this book, either directly or indirectly.

Legal Notice:
This book is copyright protected. It is only for personal use. You cannot amend, distribute, sell, use, quote or paraphrase any part, or the content within this book, without the consent of the author or publisher.

Disclaimer Notice:
Please note the information contained within this document is for educational and entertainment purposes only. All effort has been executed to present accurate, up to date, reliable, complete information. No warranties of any kind are declared or implied. Readers acknowledge that the author is not engaged in the rendering of legal, financial, medical or professional advice. The content within this book has been derived from various sources. Please consult a licensed professional before attempting any techniques outlined in this book.

By reading this document, the reader agrees that under no circumstances is the author responsible for any losses, direct or indirect, that are incurred as a result of the use of the information contained within this document, including, but not limited to, errors, omissions, or inaccuracies.

Table of Contents

Introduction 1
Chapter 1: What Is NBA Basketball? 5
  Humble Beginnings 6
    Naismith's Thirteen Rules 7
  Welcome to the NBA 9
    The Basketball Association of America 9
    The BAA-NBL Merger 11
  We're Playing Basketball 12
    The Fundamentals 12
    The Game 13
    The Players 14
Chapter 2: Greatest of All Time 19
  The Point Guards 20
    Magic Johnson 20
    Steve Nash 21
    Stephen Curry 22
  The Shooting Guards 24
    Michael Jordan 24
    Kobe Bryant 25
    Allen Iverson 27
  The Small Forwards 28
    Larry Bird 28
    Lebron James 30
    Kevin Durant 31
  The Power Forwards 33
    Dirk Nowitzki 33
    Tim Duncan 34
    Charles Barkley 36
  The Centers 37

Kareem Abdul-Jabbar 38
Shaquille O' Neal...39
David Robinson...41
G.N.O.A.T. (Greatest Nicknames of All Time) 42

Chapter 3: Top Ten Greatest Coaches 47
Number Ten: John Kundla..48
Number Nine: Jack Ramsay 50
Number Eight: Lenny Wilkens....................................51
Number Seven: Larry Brown.......................................54
Number Six: Jerry Sloan...56
Number Five: Red Auerbach 58
Number Four: Don Nelson...60
Number Three: Pat Riley..62
Number Two: Phil Jackson...64
Number One: Gregg Popovich 66

Chapter 4: Top Ten Teams in NBA History 69
Number Ten: 1966-1967 Philadelphia 76ers 69
Number Nine: 2013-2014 San Antonio Spurs 71
Number Eight: 2007-2008 Boston Celtics 72
Number Seven: 2012-2013 Miami Heat 73
Number Six: 1988-1989 Detroit Pistons 75
Number Five: 1985-1986 Boston Celtics 76
Number Four: 1986-1987 Los Angeles Lakers.............77
Number Three: 2000-2001 Los Angeles Lakers 78
Number Two: 1995-1996 Chicago Bulls 79
Number One: 2016-2017 Golden State Warriors 81

Chapter 5: NBA Trivia and Forgotten Facts.................... 83
Did You Know…? 83
The Forgotten Facts...88

Chapter 6: Inspiring Stories 93
Allen Iverson 93
Lebron James 94
Muggsy Bogues 94
Trevor Ariza...95
Michael Jordan..96

Chuck Cooper, Nat Clifton, and Earl Lloyd......................96
Magic Johnson 97
Isiah Thomas 97
Chris Andersen...98
Jimmy Butler..98

Chapter 7: Greatest Underdog Wins............................ 101
"We Believe" 102
Game Seven Heroics 103
13 in 33 104
The Biggest Comeback 105
The Undeniables..106
Linsanity 107
The Dark Horse 109
Cleveland, This is For You 111

Conclusion 113
References 119

Introduction

It all comes down to this. There are ten seconds left in the game, the score is tied, and you have the basketball. You dribble it while slowly advancing past the half-court line, and your defender eyes you carefully, waiting for you to make a move. From the corner of your eye, you see your coach shouting something. You guess he's telling your teammates to watch for the rebound if your shot misses. But you're not going to miss it. You've been practicing this exact scenario for years. Six seconds... five seconds... four seconds... now you make your move.  You shift to your right and start driving to the basket, and your opponent follows, which is precisely what you expected them to do. Quickly you plant your front foot, halting your momentum, and step back while dribbling the ball between your legs. Your opponent tries to do the same, but it's too late.

You've created space for yourself, and, with your opponent scrambling to get his footing back, you shoot your shot. The ball travels in a perfect arc as the clock winds down. Two seconds... one second... swish. Nothing but net. The buzzer sounds as the arena erupts in cheers; you raise your hands in victory as your teammates envelop you in the tightest group hug of your life. You've won the game for your team- no, not just the game, the championship. In the most exciting game seven of all time. In your rookie season. You're a prodigy, a legend, the greatest basketball player of all time.

And then everything starts to fade. The arena disappears, the crowd fades away, your teammates are gone. Now it's just you, your ball rolling onto the front lawn and the basket nailed to the top of the garage door. It's sobering, but it doesn't shake you. You love basketball, and that scenario isn't fake. It just hasn't happened yet.

Basketball has a way of making us feel bigger than we are; it's a sport that makes you feel like a superstar every time you touch the ball. This is mostly thanks to the NBA, the basketball league that creates superstars. For decades, the NBA has been the premier spot for the best basketball players in the world, launching these athletes into stardom and beyond. It has brought intense world matchups, mesmerizing plays, heart-stopping moments, and tearful memories. Memories like the one mentioned above, memories that fans have seen play out many times. Ask any fan, and they're certain to describe the moment they first started watching the NBA like it's a life-altering moment for them.

But has it always been like this? Do you know what made the NBA what it is today? In this book, you will discover the history behind those three letters, learn more about its infamous players and teams, and relive some of the greatest moments on and off the court. That's right, in your hands is an all-in-one history book about the NBA, ready to teach you all you need to know about the league that would have taken you years to learn on your own. I've been an avid sports fan all my life and have been studying sports history for many years. I love keeping the history of great sports such as basketball alive. I give this book to you in the hopes that you become as big a fan of the NBA as I am and that you become curious enough to dive in and learn more about the league. If you're ready to start your journey to become an expert on all things NBA, then keep reading. But first, let's start by answering one very important question…

Chapter 1: What Is NBA Basketball?

It's February 18th, 2022. On this cold Friday evening, the bustling city of Cleveland, Ohio, finds itself much busier than usual as it plays host to what's sure to be an exciting, athletic weekend. The best and brightest basketball players the NBA has to offer have made their way into the city to the Rocket Mortgage FieldHouse Arena in celebration of the NBA All-Star Weekend, culminating that Sunday in the 71st annual All-Star Game. For decades, this has been the spectacle in North America to watch the most talented basketball players in the world compete against each other. Not just for a notch in the win column for their team, but for major bragging rights and a chance to show off their skills in an arena filled with tens of thousands of NBA fans (including some prominent celebrities) across the globe. Every year, one city is chosen to host the event with promises of entertainment through flashy, high-octane basketball games and contests that will test a handful of players' fundamentals, shooting, and how much they can wow the audience with their innovative slam dunks.

This event serves as a snapshot of what the NBA is like today. It's not just a sport; it's a spectacle with emotional finishes, jaw-dropping moments, and great feats of athleticism. The National Basketball Association is one of the most popular sports in the United States and around the world. Top-tier athletes play amidst bright lights, flashing cameras, and screaming fans and coaches eighty-two games a year (and a little more if their team makes the playoffs). Sponsorships and advertisements are pasted across the hardwood floor, on the players' sweat-drenched jerseys, and on the Jumbotrons hanging from the arena's ceiling. Commentators sit in their booths or at their tables, narrating the events for those listening on the radio or watching the game on television. It's a thrill to watch.

But it hasn't always been like this. There hasn't always been an All-Star Weekend, eighty-two game seasons, or slam dunks. There haven't always been excited announcers exclaiming "Bang!" as the best scorer in the league knocks down a game-winning three. In fact, less than eighty years ago, there wasn't even an NBA. As we know it today, basketball has undergone a remarkable evolution, and it all started with a couple of peach baskets and a dream.

Humble Beginnings

In 1891, physical education instructor James Naismith was tasked with creating a fun game for his students to play indoors during the winter at the YMCA Training School in Springfield, Massachusetts. He decided on making up a game of his own. The first iteration of basketball drew on elements from inspiration from football, soccer, and hockey. Naismith had two peach baskets nailed to the lower rails of the balcony on either side of the gym, split his class into two equal teams, and tossed them a soccer ball. The main objective of the game: throw the ball into the other team's basket. When a team successfully did this, they earned a point (or a "goal" as it was first called), and a janitor was tasked with getting the ball out of the basket. Shortly after, they carved a small hole into the bottom of each basket so they could poke it out with a stick, and later they decided on cutting out the bottom of the basket entirely so the ball went right on through.

The new game was coined "basketball" because, simply put. It involved a basket and a ball and a stunningly simple solution compared to the names of other sports.

Soon the winter season died down, but basketball remained a regular sport played by Naismith and his class. In March of 1892, the first public basketball game was played, and its popularity quickly spread after that. The YMCA advertised the sport all around the world, American colleges latched onto it with the first recorded basketball game between two colleges occurring in 1895, during World War I. Basketball was a hit with the troops, and in 1936 (three years before James Naismith's death), basketball became an official Olympic sport.

And in 1946, the National Basketball Association was officially formed.

Naismith's Thirteen Rules

When he first invented basketball, James Naismith also came up with thirteen rules that formed the way he wanted to see the game be played. Both an umpire and a referee enforced the rules. Consider these rules and how much basketball has changed from its creation to what it's like now. Are there rules that still exist today? Are there rules you want to see come back?

1. You can throw the ball in any direction using one or both of your hands.
2. You can "bat" (swing at with your arm) the ball in any direction with one or both of your hands.
3. You *cannot* run with the ball; you must throw it from the spot where you catch it. However, discretion will be shown for someone who is running to catch the ball.
4. You cannot use your arms or body to hold the ball; it must be held in or between both of your hands.
5. You are not allowed to shoulder, hold, push, trip, or strike a person on the opposing team. Doing this once counts as a foul; twice means you're disqualified until the next goal is made.
6. You get a foul if you violate rules 3 or 4 or do anything described in rule 5.
7. If your team makes three consecutive fouls, the opposing team gets an automatic goal.
8. You get a goal when the ball is thrown or batted into the other team's basket and stays in.
9. When the ball goes out of bounds, it will be thrown in by the person that first touches it. If there's a dispute about this, the umpire will throw it in instead. The "thrower-in" has five seconds to throw the ball; if they hold it for any longer, then the ball goes to the opposing team. The umpire gives your team a foul if you intentionally delay the game.

10. The umpire judges the conduct on the field and notes the fouls; they will tell the referee when three consecutive fouls have been made.

11. The referee keeps time and judges the ball, which means they decide when it's in play, in-bounds, and which team has control of it. They also decide when a goal has been made and keep track of how many goals there have been.

12. The game is played in fifteen-minute halves with a five-minute rest in between.

13. At the end of the game, the team with the most goals wins. If there's a draw, the team captains can agree to keep going until another goal is made.

Welcome to the NBA

The NBA has quite an interesting bit of history behind it, full of opportunity, risks, and a major merger that changed the game's history forever. It's actually very apropos that we look back on how the NBA started because, at the time of this writing, the league is celebrating its 75th year of existence. So, what's changed in between those seventy-five years? How different is the NBA of today compared to its storied beginning? Well, for starters, it didn't even have the same name.

The Basketball Association of America

It's June 1946, and the owner of Boston Garden arena Walter Brown saw these major ice hockey arenas and realized that, on most nights, they were empty. What a waste! Seeing how popular basketball was in American colleges, the Olympics, and other places worldwide, Brown sought to bring that popularity into these empty arenas. Joining forces with other major ice hockey arena owners throughout the United States, they created a professional basketball league known as the Basketball Association of America (BAA). There were other leagues during this time, but what would separate the BAA from everyone else was that they would primarily play in large arenas in major cities, giving themselves and the sport greater exposure and greater profits.

The league started with eleven teams, divided into the Eastern and Western divisions. They played a sixty-game season, with each game being forty-eight minutes long instead of the customary forty minutes. Five months after the creation of the league, the BAA hosted its first game at Maple Leaf Gardens in Toronto between the Toronto Huskies and the New York Knickerbockers. The first season was... a learning experience, to say the least. The arena-only conditions were causing some problems for the league. Some owners wouldn't properly change out the floors in the hockey arenas and would just put the hardwood over the ice, resulting in warped wood and puddles all over the floor that would cancel games altogether. Some arenas weren't heated, which prompted fans to come to games wrapped in blankets and had the players using gloves. And maybe these conditions wouldn't be so bad if each arena was packed every night, but they were barely averaging three thousand fans per game. Nonetheless, they persevered, the games went on, and they moved into post-game play. In 1947, they crowned their first champions: the Philadelphia Warriors.

The league persevered through these first few years thanks in part to teams from other leagues joining them and also because they were really establishing themselves as the league for college players to turn professional. Audiences loved seeing players they'd watch in college play for their local BAA teams, and it was getting the league the exposure they needed. As the other leagues floundered, losing their money and teams, the BAA continued to grow in popularity. And then the merger happened.

The BAA-NBL Merger

From the beginning, the greatest rival of the BAA was the National Basketball League (NBL). The NBL formed in 1937, almost a decade before the BAA was even a thought in Walter Brown's mind. The rivalry between the two leagues was short but heated. It's said that while the BAA was playing in the bigger cities and arenas, the NBL was the one with the bigger stars. This, of course, would change when NBL teams started to jump ship for the increasingly popular BAA. For three years, they battled not just for players but also for fans– *especially* for fans. However, when the dust settled, the NBL was running out of money and teams, and they agreed to be absorbed into the BAA in August of 1949. This merger would create a whole new league with seventeen teams, six from the remnants of the NBL, and a changed name. They would be known as the National Basketball Association from there on out. And though the modern-day NBA considers the history and statistics of the BAA as its own, the NBL left its own lasting influence on the league. In fact, five current NBA teams can trace their history all the way back to the NBL:

1. The Minneapolis Lakers, now known as the Los Angeles Lakers.
2. The Rochester Royals, now known as the Sacramento Kings.
3. The Fort Wayne Zollner Pistons, now known as the Detroit Pistons.

4. The Buffalo Bisons/Tri-Cities Blackhawks, now known as the Atlanta Hawks.
5. The Syracuse Nationals, now known as the Philadelphia 76ers.

We're Playing Basketball

If James Naismith could see how much basketball has evolved since 1891, I wonder what he would think? Would he mourn the loss of the peach baskets? What about the soccer ball or the umpire? Nowadays, with the advent of dribbling, people can move up and down the court with the ball as long as they keep bouncing it, and instead of one point per shot, you can get two, three, and maybe even four points if you're lucky. There's a fluidity to the game that allows for creativity and quick-thinking to shine just as much as athleticism and strength. You get the best of a few worlds now with basketball. Let's look at how the game is played now. What do you think will change about it in the future?

The Fundamentals

There are certain things you're always going to see on the court, no matter if it's a pick-up game at the park or game seven of the NBA Finals. These are the fundamentals of basketball: the ball, the hoop, and the court. Basketball is now used to define the sport itself and the ball you use to play it. Instead of a soccer ball, you now have this inflated rubber ball that's typically orange and has bumps and dark, circular lines across the surface. It's got a very distinct sound when you bounce it. The hoop is what you throw the ball into; it's a metal ring with a webbed cover of yarn typically suspended from the bottom, and behind it is a board made of wood or glass called the backboard. It keeps the hoop secure, and you can bounce the ball off it to get a better shot at scoring. And lastly, there's the court. Basketball has traveled out of the gym and can now be played pretty much anywhere you have a ball and a hoop. The court is what you're playing on, whether that's the classic hardwood flooring of a gym, the asphalt at the park, or the concrete of your driveway. Though the materials have evolved, the fundamentals have remained relatively the same. You're ready to play some basketball as long as you've got a ball, hoop, and court.

The Game

How basketball is played is where the most change has happened. No longer do you need to stay in one place if you have the ball. Now, you can bounce it (dribbling), throw it over to

an open teammate (passing), or take a chance at throwing it into the hoop (shooting). The game now plays at a quickened, more fluid pace with the advent of these three moves, though fouls still exist and breaks in the form of "time-outs" help to break the constant flow of action. The umpire is now gone, and their duties have been given to the referee who remains. You

still see the inspiration from other sports in this modern version of basketball. Free throws after a foul are akin to the penalty kicks in soccer, specific plays can be called by the coaches and relayed to their team just like in football, and defenders can block your shots just like in hockey. Basketball is a mental sport just as much as it is physical. More strategy is involved, more movement is called for to get past defenders on the opposite team, more opportunities are given to score points.

Speaking of opportunities, players have come up with so many moves over the years in order to make more opportunities for themselves to score. You have dribble moves like the crossover and the step back to create space from your defender so you can take an open shot. You've got no-look passes and alley-oops to get the ball to one of your teammates without the other team even seeing it. And of course, you've got the slam dunk, which makes it so you don't even have to throw the ball if you're close enough to the hoop. You just need to jump and put it in. The creativity of the players has made basketball so much more exciting and rewarding to watch.

The Players

When basketball grew in popularity, it attracted a diverse range of people to the sport. Soon, you had people of varying heights and builds on the court, and it didn't make sense that everyone was playing the same role. When you look at a sport like football, every person on the team has a position they play that accurately showcases their abilities; it only made sense that basketball would do this too. A "position" is a term used to describe ways to distinguish and delegate certain responsibilities to your teammates on the court; that way, you wouldn't have someone that's seven feet tall zipping around defenders trying to catch a pass and shoot from the three-point line. Traditional, organized basketball has two teams with five players each on the court at all times, and each of those five players takes on a different position.

First, there's the "point guard." They're typically the most agile person on your team who has both quick feet and an even quicker mind. They advance the ball up the court to their team's side and set up their team's offense, calling plays or audibles, and getting the ball to whoever it needs to go. Compared to football, they're like the quarterback of the team. Point guards need to be observant of everyone on the court. They need to know where their teammates are and where they're going to be depending on the play called, and they also need to be wary of where the defense is and how much they're paying attention. They do all this thinking while also ensuring the ball doesn't get stolen right out from under them. On defense, their job is usually to defend the other team's point guard and try to disrupt the play as best as they can. All five positions are given a number on the court; the point guard is known as number one.

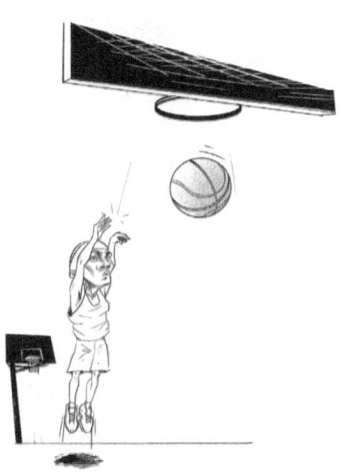

The number two position belongs to the "shooting guard." This is one of the most reliable shooters on your team, the one you can trust to score a basket from nearly anywhere on the court. That means they need to be just as fast and agile as the point guard, maybe even more since you can draw up a lot of plays for them. They need to be able to shoot far from the basket, at midrange, near the hoop, and anywhere else the play needs them to be. On defense, they're like a fly that won't go away; they slip past bigger defenders and travel around the court trying to disrupt plays and keep the other team's shooters from getting open.

Next, we have the "small forward." The number three spot is the most versatile of any of the positions and the one that arguably demands the most amount of skill. You want to get the best of both worlds with the small forward because they need to be athletic enough to move around the court and make shots from a wide range of distance, but you also want them to be tall and strong so they can play tough defense and help with grabbing rebounds (missed shots from the other team).

At number four, we have the "power forward." Their purpose is right there in the name. They're one of the most powerful forces you can have out on the court due to their size and strength. Their length makes them a threat near the basket on both the offensive and defensive end; they can score the ball just as well as they can keep from getting scored on. However, they still need to retain some quickness, as they need to take a reliable jump shot (especially from midrange) and guard against opponents shooting from the midrange.

Taking the five spot is the "center." They are the anchor of your team, the tallest and strongest force you have, the big man near the basket. You won't typically find the center out on the midrange or three-point line, and neither should you expect that. The center lives near the basket and will use a variety of moves in their arsenal to get past their defender and score, or they'll pass the ball back out to an open teammate. On defense, they're somewhat akin to a goalie because they make sure no one gets near the net; when a shot misses, they're the ones most likely to get the rebound.

Today, these positions take on a more diverse set of responsibilities and are sometimes asked to work on shots outside the comfort zone (this is known as 'stretching the floor'). You'll have coaches asking power forwards to develop a three-point shot or for their shooting guard to run the ball up the court. Centers can sometimes be the size of power forwards or even small forwards if the coach wants to use a 'small ball' lineup, where they sacrifice size for speed in order to outrun and outshoot the other team. Regardless of what changes are made, the core of each position remains the same. Each person on the team has a position that fits them best and can thrive with responsibilities that others on their team can't, and whether they're the point guard or the center, they're all important to the team's success.

Chapter 2: Greatest of All Time

In celebration of seventy-five years of helping to bring basketball into the mainstream and making it a top sport throughout the world, the NBA released a list of who they consider to be some of the greatest basketball players of all time. This list is known as the NBA 75th Anniversary Team, and despite the name, there are actually seventy-six players on the list due to a tie in voting. This list was decided on by a selected committee of media members, coaches, general managers, team executives, and also players that were once or still are in the league. On this list are a plethora of All-Star caliber players, NBA champions, and recipients of prestigious awards such as the Most Valuable Player (MVP) award. They represent the best the NBA has had to offer in the seventy-five years of its existence.

But who is the greatest basketball player of all time? Well, that's been a serious topic of debate for decades and will most likely continue to be debated years from now. There's so much criteria to look through when considering who to place as the "Greatest of All Time" (or G.O.A.T.) like how many championships they've won, how much they've scored, whether or not they were a good teammate, and also what kind of impact/lasting legacy they left on the league. If you asked any random person who they thought was the G.O.A.T. of the NBA, you'd get a different answer every time. In this chapter, we're going to look at three players from all five positions and show just how much they brought to the game of basketball. All fifteen of these players made a significant impact in the NBA. Who do you think is the greatest of all time?

The Point Guards

We'll first look at the floor generals, the ones who command the court and make each play look so effortlessly done. Point guards have given the NBA some of the flashiest passes and most clutch moments in the face of insurmountable odds. Here are three of the best.

Honorable Mentions: Damian Lillard, Chris Paul, Isiah Thomas, Gilbert Arenas, Nate "Tiny" Archibald

Magic Johnson

Earvin "Magic" Johnson was the number one pick in the 1979 NBA Draft, going to the Los Angeles Lakers with whom he would stay for his entire career. Magic was already a star coming out of college, and he carried that talent into his NBA career, becoming one of the very few people to ever make the NBA Finals in his rookie season. Who could ever forget his performance in game six of the 1980 finals when he replaced an injured Kareem Abdul-Jabbar at the center position? Even though he was six-foot-nine. Far from being center height, he still put up a great stat line of forty-two points, fifteen rebounds, and seven assists to help the Lakers win the series and win himself the award for Finals MVP, the *only* rookie ever to win that award.

Throughout his career, Magic Johnson was known not just for his efficient scoring but also his flashy passes. He'd beat everyone up the floor, upping the tempo, and would pass the ball out to a teammate that no one else saw but him. Or he'd take the ball himself, slip past his defenders and attack the basket for easy points. He'd gotten the nickname "Magic" in high school, and every time he was on the court, he would live up to it; everything he did was magic. He beat opponents physically *and* mentally, dominating the league for a decade straight. Sadly, his career was cut short due to an HIV diagnosis in 1991 that forced him to retire. By the end of his career, he'd earned five NBA Championships, three MVP and Finals MVP awards, ten thousand recorded assists, and at the time of this writing, he still holds the record for most assists per game at 11.2.

Steve Nash

Steve Nash is widely considered to be one of the greatest basketball players to have never won an NBA Championship, though it certainly wasn't for lack of trying. On any night, especially in his prime, Steve Nash could be the most efficient player on the court, scarily accurate in both his passing *and* shooting. He was a truly elite player who maybe deserves more praise than people give him. Save for the people in Phoenix, Arizona, who still consider him a hero.

He began his career with the Phoenix Suns as the fifteenth pick in the 1996 NBA Draft, though his time there was short-lived… for now. After a couple of seasons, he was traded to the Dallas Mavericks, where he really started to come into his own. By his fourth season there, he was averaging eighteen points, eight assists, and at least one steal per game; he'd also been voted into the All-Star Game that year and was a driving force in the Mavericks making it all the way to the Western Conference Finals. When he became a free agent in 2004, he returned to the Phoenix Suns, where he helped bolster their infamous "Seven Seconds or Less" offensive style. The style required the team to get the ball up the court and find a good shot as fast as possible before the defense could even set up. This would require a point guard with a quick enough mind to make the right calls and passes under pressure, and that's what Steve Nash did best.

His second stint with the Suns is what cemented him as a star and one of the greatest point guards of his generation. His playmaking ability carried the fast-paced offense, and his accurate and stunning passes (which he credits to his experience playing soccer) ensured he'd almost always find an open man. Not only that, but he could be a threat shooting-wise as well. He knew how to pick his shots on the outside and used his footwork to lose his defender and get to the hoop. He led this version of the Suns to the playoffs five times and the Western Conference Finals three times.

After nineteen years in the NBA, Steve Nash finally retired at the end of the 2014-2015 season. In that time, he had amassed two MVP awards, eight appearances at the NBA All-Star Game, and led the league in assists five times. At the time of this writing, he is currently the head coach for the Brooklyn Nets.

Stephen Curry

If there's one man that best defines the modern NBA landscape, it's Stephen Curry. Right now, he's still an active player for the Golden State Warriors, but with everything he's accomplished so far, he will no doubt go down as one of the greatest point guards of all time. He was selected seventh in the 2009 NBA Draft by Golden State, putting up modest numbers for a team that, well, to say they were mediocre would be an understatement. He was good, but people were close to writing him off due to his history of injuries, especially with his ankles. But that's just the origin story for the evolution of Steph Curry. As his body grew stronger and more durable, his game had shown significant improvement as well. He would hone one part of his game to be the deadliest weapon: his three-point shooting.

When you saw his name, you immediately imagined him taking a three-point shot at an impossible distance and making it look as easy as a lay-up. This is his calling card. He's not only known for taking a great volume of three-point shots but also for taking them seemingly anywhere on the court with deadly accuracy. When Curry has the ball in his hands, nowhere is safe. If you give him even an inch of space, he will take advantage of that and shoot the ball with great ease. His stellar shooting performances helped lead the Golden State Warriors to three NBA championships in a five-year span.

Curry and the Warriors have changed the game. Perimeter defense has become a major emphasis for coaches. Players are more spaced out and are encouraged to widen their shooting range, and teams are attempting twice the number of three-pointers they used to before Curry joined the league. With a little more than a decade of experience under his belt, there's still more time for Stephen Curry's legacy to grow, but three NBA Championships, two MVP awards, and a hand in changing the landscape of basketball are some impressive accolades already.

The Shooting Guards

These men are the highlights of any highlight reel, the shot-makers, and risk-takers. The shooting guards on any team are game-changing, and these three men certainly had a hand in changing the game.

Honorable Mentions: James Harden, Reggie Miller, Tracy McGrady, Vince Carter, Dwyane Wade

Michael Jordan

You're always going to get a different answer when you ask who the G.O.A.T. is, but there's one name you might hear more than most. Michael Jordan is one of, if not *the* most popular basketball players of all time. He was the poster child for the NBA in the 90s, one of the leading stars in *Space Jam*, the logo for a prolific sneaker brand, and oh yeah, he's also *really* good at basketball. One of the best. He entered the league as the number three pick in the 1984 Draft for the Chicago Bulls. Back then, the NBA was the land of the giants, offenses revolved around the power forwards and centers, and Jordan went right to work slaying those giants.

What set Michael Jordan apart from the other players in the league was his athleticism and mental fortitude. On his worst day, he could still outrun, out-jump, and out-play everyone on the other team; many credit this to his fundamentals; he made the basics look spectacular. He had an unbeatable jump shot, and should he choose to get into the post, he'd use his footwork to make the defense dizzy and drive in for a quick lay-up or dunk. He was confident in his game, but his competitiveness drove him to become the greatest. Every game for him was a "win at all costs" scenario. Who could ever forget game five of the 1997 Finals when Michael Jordan entered the game while battling a nasty case of the flu. He was dehydrated and could barely keep himself up, but he still scored thirty-eight points and led his team to victory. Speaking of the Finals, that's where he seemed to shine the most. In his six appearances at the NBA Finals, Jordan and the Bulls won all six times. By the end of his storied career, he had amassed six NBA championships, five MVP awards, a Defensive Player of the Year award, and currently holds the record for highest points-per-game average at 30.1 points.

Kobe Bryant

There are very few players in the NBA that have the talent to skip college and go straight to the league after high school; Kobe Bryant was one such player. Coming into the league, some were already considering him to be the next Michael Jordan, and for all intents and purposes, he lived up to those expectations and then some. Kobe modeled a lot of his game after Jordan, and you can see that especially in his footwork,

jump shot, and his ability to close out games. Kobe excelled in making the hard shots when they counted the most. A couple of things separate Kobe's game from Jordan's; he had a better three-point shot percentage, and his mental fortitude was on a completely different level. The game never seemed to end for Kobe, basketball was always first and foremost on his mind, and he spent every minute he could getting better and better. His unwavering commitment for the game, the drive to be the best with no excuses, is a mindset that has been dubbed the "Mamba Mentality." Players today try to emulate this mindset, hoping to be the player Kobe was from his first game to his last.

The story of Kobe Bryant in the NBA starts in the 1996 NBA Draft, where the Los Angeles Lakers had traded their starting center Vlade Divac to the Charlotte Hornets for the thirteenth pick in the draft. With that pick, the Hornets chose Kobe for the Lakers. Kobe would remain a Laker for his entire twenty-year career. A few years into the league, he secured his spot as the second-best player on the team next to center Shaquille O' Neal as the duo helped bring the team three straight championships. When O'Neal left the team in 2004, critics wondered if Kobe could truly step up and be the leader the Lakers needed, and for the rest of his career, he proved he could. A few years later, he would lead the Lakers to two more championships, and, on the quest for a sixth ring, he ran his body ragged. Injuries plagued him the last couple of years of his career until he finally declared that he would retire at the end of the 2015-2016 season. He led his team to one more victory in his very last game while scoring sixty points. Kobe left the league with five NBA championships, two NBA Finals MVP awards, eighteen All-Star Game appearances, two Olympic gold medals, and holds the record for the second-most points scored in a single game at eighty-one points. Tragically,

Kobe Bryant and his daughter died in a helicopter accident in January 2020.

Allen Iverson

Another player to add to the list of the greatest to play the game without ever winning a championship, Allen Iverson was iconic on and off the court. He carried himself with

so much confidence and swagger and talked a big game to anyone who would listen. But he could always back it up when his shoes hit the hardboard. Allen Iverson (A.I.) had a play style that was fast-paced and mesmerizing, backed up by his impressive ball-handling and shooting skills. He personified the isolation style (iso ball) of the early 2000s. He seemingly turned the game into a one-on-one situation, choosing to get no help from his teammates to out-play their defender and score the ball.

A.I. would continuously win these battles due to his aforementioned ball-handling skills that helped him hone his signature move: the crossover. Using his quick feet and hands, Iverson would fake going one way before switching the ball to his other hand and shifting his feet to go the other way. Done right, his opponent would sometimes trip over himself trying to change direction.

Allen Iverson is most synonymous with the Philadelphia 76ers, who drafted him with the number one pick in the 1996 NBA Draft. He immediately made an impact on the court, becoming one of their leading scoring options and winning the rookie of the Year award. Despite being six feet tall, which is a below-average height in NBA standards, he could score over anybody and proved it by winning the NBA scoring title four times in his first nine years in the league. He led the Sixers to five playoff appearances and one trip to the NBA Finals. Attitude issues eventually ended his ten-year run with the Sixers, as he was traded to the Denver Nuggets in the middle of the 2005-2006 season. Unfortunately, he would never find the same level of success at this point of his career as he had with the Sixers, and his production regressed. He spent the rest of his NBA career playing on four different teams (one of them being in a Turkish basketball league) before officially retiring from basketball in 2013. His accolades include one MVP award, a Rookie of the Year award, and eleven All-Star game appearances.

The Small Forwards

This "Swiss Army Knife" of the team is the one who can do it all. The small forward position might be the most demanding of the five positions, but if the player can take the responsibility, then they have long, fruitful careers ahead of them. Here are three of the greatest.

Honorable Mentions: Scottie Pippen, Paul Pierce, Carmelo Anthony, Julius Erving, James Worthy

Larry Bird

The 1980s were defined by one of the greatest basketball rivalries of all-time between the Boston Celtics and the Los Angeles Lakers. The Lakers had their fair share of stars during this time, but when you look at the Celtics, you have one constant that would hold his own against them all: Larry Bird. Dubbed the "Great

White Hope" and "Larry Legend," Bird was a man who could seemingly do it all on the court. He wasn't the most athletic person on the court, but that usually never mattered because he had a mind for the game that could beat any defender at any time. He could shoot from anywhere, pass the ball through the hands of the opposing team, trash-talked on the court, and was essential during crunch time. Larry Bird would do anything you asked of him, no questions asked and with no hesitation. He was a winner, and he made the Celtics winners.

Larry Bird's career started as the sixth pick in the 1978 NBA Draft by the Boston Celtics, with whom he would stay for the entirety of his time in the league. He actually started out playing as a power forward, but his versatility meant that he could play both forward positions. Whether he played the three or four, Larry Bird remained the number one option for his team. Much like Magic Johnson, one of his ultimate rivals, Bird immediately improved his team and led them all the way to the playoffs in his rookie year. Unfortunately, they were defeated in the Eastern Conference Finals. Regardless, he and the Celtics persevered and eventually made it to the NBA Finals five times throughout the 80s. He may have had a much longer career, but the other stars on these Celtics teams were in their last good years, which meant he had to put a lot of the team's production on himself. This caused him major back and foot issues that caused him to retire after thirteen years. Aside from helping to revitalize the NBA during a rough time, Larry Bird is also credited with three NBA championships, three MVP awards, twelve All-Star Game appearances, and one Olympic gold medal.

Lebron James

As long as basketball exists, the list of people who could conceivably be the G.O.A.T. grows. One man who's making an  all-time case for themselves is Lebron James. Nineteen years into his career, he's amassed a legend that rivals Kobe and Jordan, to whom he's been compared constantly. He was drafted straight out of his school, just like Kobe, with the first pick in the 2003 NBA Draft by his hometown team, the Cleveland Cavaliers. Just like Jordan, he's been the most popular player in the league, and he's starred in the sequel to Space Jam entitled *Space Jam: A New Legacy*. However, when he's on the court, he takes his legend into his own hands. Currently, in his nineteenth year in the NBA, Lebron is finally showing signs of slowing down, but his production level is still mind-blowing. This is due to his excellent conditioning and versatile play style that allows him to play at pretty much any position. And it's that versatility that makes him the definition of a small forward. He can score from anywhere on the court and has a motor that he knows when to turn on in order to drive to the basket for an emphatic dunk or chase a defender down to get a block. Later in his career, he improved his court awareness, allowing him to find open teammates better and get easy assists.

One of his most remarkable skills is his ability to lead any team he's been on impressive postseason runs, no matter how bad the team was. And he's been on some historically bad teams. In just his third year with the Cleveland Cavaliers, he'd begin his postseason legacy by taking his team to the second round of the playoffs. The following season, he took the team all the way to the NBA Finals, which included an impressive comeback victory in game five of the Eastern Conference Finals against the Pistons. Though he led the Cavaliers to more playoff berths, this was where he'd peak with them… for now. Lebron would find his most tremendous postseason success with the Miami Heat, who he joined in 2010 to form a "big three" with Chris Bosh and Dwyane Wade. He went to the NBA Finals in all five years he was with the team, winning a championship three of those times. In 2014, he decided to return to Cleveland in the hopes of winning a championship with his hometown team. With a better-built team, Lebron went to the NBA Finals four more times in wars with the Golden State Warriors; he accomplished his mission in the 2015-2016 season when Cleveland won the NBA championship. In 2018, he ended his second stint with Cleveland and opted to join the Los Angeles Lakers in free agency, where he remains at the time of this writing. Things have been shaky, to say the least, and yet he was still able to win another championship with them during the 2019-2020 season. It's uncertain when he'll officially call it a career, but what he's accomplished is already phenomenal. Right now, "King James" holds four NBA championships, four MVP awards, eighteen appearances in the All-Star game, two Olympic gold medals, and the record for all-time points in the playoffs.

Kevin Durant

When you talk about how flexible every position in basketball affords today, you can't do so without mentioning Kevin Durant. Standing at almost seven feet tall with just as impressive of a wingspan, you would think he'd be slotted right into the center position or maybe even a power forward. But instead, he's a small forward, perhaps even the best one currently playing. He handles himself like a guard and has the fundamentals to back it up, and his length makes him nearly impossible to block if you're matched up with him. He has exploited this to become one of the best scorers in the game. He's unstoppable across the floor, reliable in the clutch, and good on defense as well; in other words, he's the total package.

His career began in the 2007 NBA Draft when he was chosen at number two by the Seattle Supersonics, who would become the Oklahoma City Thunder in a couple of years. Those Thunder teams with Durant, Russell Westbrook, and James Harden played some of the most exciting basketball around. Five years later, that young team would make it all the way to the 2012 NBA Finals before eventually falling to the Miami Heat. The Thunder remained playoff contenders and sometimes even the favorites to win it all. Durant and the Thunder never made it back to the finals due to injuries, shake-ups in the roster, and an incredibly strong Western Conference. He joined the Golden State Warriors in free agency in a rather controversial move. Not only were the Warriors the most dominant team in the league, but they had also beaten the Thunder in the playoffs that year. Joining them felt like Durant was taking the "easy road" to a championship. Regardless if that's true or not, Durant followed the Warriors to two consecutive wins in the NBA Finals. He is now a member of the Brooklyn Nets and continues to be the number one scoring option for their team. Time will tell where Durant takes his career next, but he's already accomplished enough in his career to net him as one of the greatest small forwards of all time. Right now, he holds two NBA championships, one MVP award, two Finals MVP awards, and ten All-Star game appearances.

The Power Forwards

We finally move to the land of the giants. No matter what era, teams will always find value in the tall, athletic men who can make a jump shot just as well as they can finesse their way into a lay-up. Here are some of the greatest power forwards of all time.

Honorable Mentions: Kevin Garnett, Karl Malone, Dennis Rodman, Pau Gasol, Marc Gasol, Chris Webber

Dirk Nowitzki

When you talk about "stretching the floor," Dirk Nowitzki excelled in this. He'll go down in history as one of the hardest working basketball players in history. Though he was gifted with a seven-foot-frame, he did not possess the strength at first to be considered a force in the post or anywhere else from short range. In fact, he was deemed "soft" when coming into the league. Nowitzki fought through all of that criticism to become one of the most prolific shooters and ball-handlers in the power forward position. He struggled with getting the rebound and  defending the bigger and stronger power forwards, but he made them all look like fools on offense. He shot a career thirty-eight percent from the three-point line, averaged over twenty points per game, and had a seemingly unblockable one-legged fadeaway jumper in his arsenal. Defenders would always be weary when Dirk would try to back them up, and then one way or another, he'd catch them sleeping. He'd spin around, lean back with one leg in the air, and arc a shot that almost always found its way into the basket.

The big man from Germany was chosen in the 1998 NBA Draft as the ninth pick by the Milwaukee Bucks; however, a same-day trade saw him going to the Dallas Mavericks instead. He would stay with them his entire career. After a discouraging rookie season, Dirk was nearly ready to call it quits, but with the support of his teammate Steve Nash, he kept moving forward. He showed significant improvement in his second season, and he helped lead the Mavericks to the playoffs in his third season. They'd continue to make the playoffs each year, but it wasn't until 2006 when they finally made it all the way to the NBA Finals. However, they'd lose in six games to the Miami Heat. Dirk faced heavy criticism for his lack of leadership and inconsistency in the playoffs, but he powered through and became the leader the Mavericks needed him to be. Five years later, the Mavericks would make it all the way to the NBA Finals one more time to face a familiar foe in the Heat, who at this point had acquired their "Big Three" of Bosh, Wade, and James. Playing the best basketball of his career, Dirk fearlessly faced Miami's three-headed dragon, and six games later, he had led the Mavericks to their first championship in franchise history. Dirk would stay with the team for the rest of his career, and though they would never reach those heights again, he cemented himself as one of the greatest power forwards of all time and certainly one of the greatest players to wear a Mavericks jersey. When he officially retired, Dirk Nowitzki had acquired one NBA championship, one Finals MVP award, one MVP award, and fourteen appearances at the All-Star game.

Tim Duncan

At the same time that Dirk was coming into his own in Dallas, there was another big man just up the road in San Antonio who was making a name for himself too. Tim Duncan is a man of few words and many accolades, and he epitomized what it meant to be a power forward in the 2000s and early 2010s. He wasn't the flashiest player by any means, but what he lacked in showmanship he made up for in his amazing technical prowess on the court. He was another one of those players that fine-tuned the basics of basketball that he was unstoppable on both offense and defense. He had an amazing bank shot, grabbed rebounds effortlessly, was never selfish with the ball, and stepped up in the clutch when he needed to. He had such a mellow and sheltered personality; he kept to himself a lot which, ironically, is what made him such a popular player. His humility, consistency, and basketball knowledge earned him a long and fruitful career.

Tim Duncan never missed the postseason from his rookie season in 1997 as the number one pick by the San Antonio Spurs to his final season in 2016. He had a great support system around him, including Spurs head coach Gregg Popovich and fellow big man David Robinson. Together, he and Robinson formed the "Twin Towers" due to their tall stature and excellent defense close to the basket, and they both led the Spurs to two NBA championships before Robinson retired in 2003. By then, Duncan had matured and was molded into the leader the Spurs needed him to be, and he acquired more legendary teammates like Tony Parker and Manu Ginobli to continue their next decade and a half of playoff runs. With a solid team and a great coach, Duncan would win three more championships in the rest of his career, his last one coming in 2014 when age and injuries were about to creep up on him and slow him down. With the Spurs' future secured, Duncan called it a career at the end of 2015-2016, putting up impressive and consistent numbers until the end. He quietly accrued five NBA championships, three Finals MVP awards, two MVP awards, and eight appearances on the NBA All-Defensive First Team.

Charles Barkley

Some readers might know this man better as the blunt, brash, and hilarious analyst for NBA on TNT, but before that, he was a fantastic player that carved a name for himself in the uber-competitive 90s era of the NBA. It's rare that a player becomes the franchise player for a team, and Barkley achieved that with two teams. Barkley was a beast in the post, on both offense and defense. He was a little shorter than most power forwards during that time, but that allowed him to outmaneuver his bigger adversaries to get straight to the basket. And his height never mattered much on defense, considering he averaged twelve rebounds per game throughout his career. He made up for what he lacked in height with an aggressive playstyle and the strength to always get where he needed to be. And unlike other power forwards during his time, Barkley could even run a fastbreak. His outspoken attitude, penchant for getting into fights, and brazen opinions might be why he's better remembered nowadays, but we should never forget the top-notch player behind those words.

In 1984, he was drafted with the fifth pick by the Philadelphia 76ers, joining a team with established yet aging stars in Julius Erving and Moses Malone. He improved quickly under the watchful eye of these veterans, especially Malone, and in his second year in the league, he became the starting power forward for the team. He was a rebounding machine and one of their leading scorers, and just a few short years later, he became the leader of the Sixers when Malone was traded, and Erving retired. If the league wasn't so stacked around this time, Barkley and the Sixers might have won a championship or two. But their playoff performances never amounted to that, and in 1992 Barkley demanded a trade. He'd get his wish when he was traded to the Phoenix Suns. In the four years he played with the Suns, Barkley was their star player and led them to the playoffs every year, including an NBA Finals appearance in the 1992-1993 season against the Chicago Bulls. Wanting one last shot at winning a championship, he joined the Houston Rockets to play alongside legends Hakeem Olajuwon and Clyde Drexler. However, injuries began plaguing him this late into his career, and the best this team could do together was lose in the Western Conference Finals. He would officially retire in April 2000, having never won a championship but nonetheless leaving a big impact on the game. He achieved one MVP award, eleven appearances in the All-Star Game, one All-Star Game MVP award, and two Olympic gold medals.

The Centers

Last but not least are the mountains of the NBA landscape, the giants who roamed the land, the fifth man on every team who makes arguably the biggest difference. There have been so many unique centers throughout the years, here are just three of them.

Honorable Mentions: Hakeem Olajuwon, Dwight Howard, Wilt Chamberlain, Patrick Ewing, Yao Ming

Kareem Abdul-Jabbar

Players are rarely able to play twenty seasons in the NBA; it's even rarer that they're able to maintain a level of greatness in all twenty of those seasons. Kareem Abdul-Jabbar did both of these things. In the 70s and 80s, there wasn't a player as undeniable as Kareem, a man who was already a beast in college before making it into the league. At seven-foot two, he towered over the competition literally and figuratively, he played with amazing finesse and athleticism for a big man, and when he started aging, he still had an amazing mind for the game that propelled him. Pair that with his infamous skyhook shot, where he'd leap into the air and throw the ball into the basket with a hook-like motion, and there's no question why he too can be considered the greatest of all time.

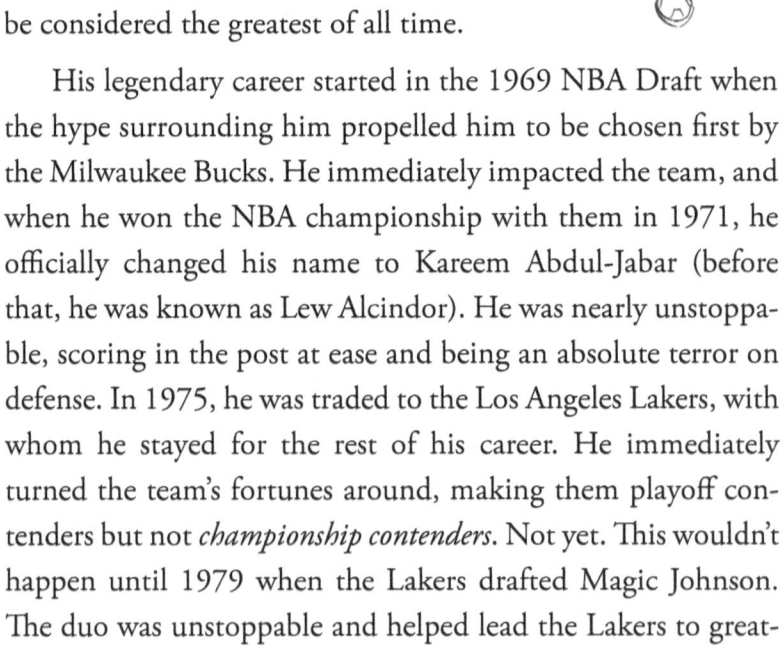

His legendary career started in the 1969 NBA Draft when the hype surrounding him propelled him to be chosen first by the Milwaukee Bucks. He immediately impacted the team, and when he won the NBA championship with them in 1971, he officially changed his name to Kareem Abdul-Jabar (before that, he was known as Lew Alcindor). He was nearly unstoppable, scoring in the post at ease and being an absolute terror on defense. In 1975, he was traded to the Los Angeles Lakers, with whom he stayed for the rest of his career. He immediately turned the team's fortunes around, making them playoff contenders but not *championship contenders*. Not yet. This wouldn't happen until 1979 when the Lakers drafted Magic Johnson. The duo was unstoppable and helped lead the Lakers to greatness in the 80s. They made it to the NBA finals eight times and won five championships in the process. At the end of the 1988 Finals, Kareem announced he would retire after the following season. His retirement tour was an emotional one; he received standing ovations at home and away games, received a yacht named "Captain Skyhook," and in his final regular-season game, every one of his teammates went on the court wearing his trademark game goggles. Kareem left the NBA with his legacy secured, along with six NBA championships, two Finals MVP awards, six MVP awards, and nineteen All-Star Game appearances.

Shaquille O' Neal

While height is undoubtedly an essential component in being a top-tier center, size matters just as much. And there's certainly no center that exemplifies this more than Shaquille O' Neal. At seven feet tall, Shaq already towered over many competitors, but when you combine that with the fact that he weighed more than three hundred pounds, and you have what amounts to the perfect storm. That is exactly what it felt like playing against Shaq. Sometimes all you could do was hold on for dear life and hope he didn't wipe you out. He used his physical frame to bully his way to the rim at every possession; weaker defenders were easily out-muscled as he laid the ball up or dunked it in. The only realistic chance you had at stopping him was if you fouled him and sent him to the free-throw line (he was notoriously bad at making his free throws). Nonetheless, it was clear that if

Shaq had the ball, you either got out of the way or ran the risk of being on the wrong end of a highlight play.

Shaq's career began as the first pick in the 1992 NBA Draft by the Orlando Magic. His impact was immediately felt as he had one of the most impressive rookie seasons ever. He was voted Player of the Week in his first week in the league, voted into the All-Star game as a starter, and was inevitably voted as the rookie of the year. Shaq wasn't just the best player on the team; he was one of the best players in the entire NBA. He was able to do what no one else had in the 90s, and that was to beat Michael Jordan and the Chicago Bulls in the playoffs. When he joined the Los Angeles Lakers in free agency in 1996, he was undoubtedly the best center in the league, but despite his efforts, the team didn't have the right pieces to make deep runs in the playoffs. The pieces finally fell for them in 1999 when Phil Jackson was hired as a head coach, and Kobe Bryant started coming into his own as a player. The Lakers won three straight NBA championships from 2000 to 2002, thanks in big part to the big man. Disputes with the front office, mostly about his salary, caused Shaq to be traded in 2004 to the Miami Heat, where he paired up with another star shooting guard, Dwyane Wade. In his second year with the team, he and Wade led them to an NBA championship. This would be the final championship of Shaq's career; though he played for many more years in the league, injuries and age had started creeping up on him, and his inability to stay in shape saw him regress. After his stint with the Heat was over, he played for the Phoenix Suns, Cleveland Cavaliers, and finally the Boston Celtics before calling it a career in June 2011. It was rough seeing him in his later years, but in his prime, there was no player like Shaquille O' Neal; he was untouchable. He received four NBA championships, an MVP award, three All-Star Game MVP awards, a Rookie of the Year award, and one Olympic gold medal.

David Robinson

We cap off our look at some of the greatest players of all time with a man who could be considered a sleeper choice for that title. David Robinson was a phenomenal center who might not get the recognition he deserves nowadays, even though he gave so much to the NBA on and off the court. Robinson was quick and agile for someone that was seven-foot-one that was a threat anywhere on the floor. He dominated on  defense, grabbing rebounds and blocking shots with ease, and on offense, his jumper was unstoppable, and he wasn't afraid to use his athleticism to drive to the hoop for an easy dunk. He was a professional, doing whatever his team asked of him and leading them to great success, and he was also a philanthropist. Robinson worked tirelessly within the community and once donated nine million dollars to help with the construction of a school in San Antonio called The Carver Academy. He set an example worthy of following in basketball and in life.

Robinson's career would have started when he was drafted first by the San Antonio Spurs in the 1987 NBA Draft; however, he was already committed to serving with the Navy and couldn't join the team for another couple of years. His military service is actually what gained him the nickname "The Admiral." When he finally joined the league in the 1989-1990 season, his impact was immediate (just like it's been for most of the greats). Through his efforts, Robinson transformed the Spurs- who had posted the worst record in the league the season prior- into near championship contenders. The twenty-four-year-old rookie took them all the way to the Western Conference semifinals, and if it wasn't for a heartbreaking loss in game seven to the Portland Trail Blazers, they could have gone even further. Injuries hindered further chances of greatness, and it was clear that the Spurs needed him for their continued success. In the 1996-1997 season, which Robinson missed most of due to a back injury, the Spurs sunk back down to a record of 20-62. However, that season nabbed them Tim Duncan, and with the "Twin Towers" formed, Robinson and the Spurs were able to win two championships finally. The first was in 1999, and the second was during his final year in 2003. Robinson had the privilege of ending his career on top, officially retiring after the Spurs beat the New Jersey Nets in six games. Would we have seen more championship greatness from The Admiral if it weren't for the injuries that plagued him? We'll never know. But he still had an amazing career, finishing with two NBA championships, an MVP award, the rookie of the Year award, and six appearances in the All-Star game. He also has a plaque in his honor given to players who win the NBA Community Assist Award.

G.N.O.A.T. (Greatest Nicknames of All Time)

Nicknames have always been a big thing in sports, and in basketball, they're everywhere. The best nicknames always have the best stories, be they endearing, inspiring, or downright hilarious. They're also catchy and original, something that takes more effort than just using someone's initials or shortening their first name. We've talked about a couple of nicknames already (King James, The Admiral, Magic Johnson), but here are more of the greatest, funniest, and most interesting ones throughout NBA history.

Air Jordan: Given to Michael Jordan due to the way he could seemingly glide through the air to make a basket.

Agent Zero: The nickname of Gilbert Arenas, referencing his jersey number and ability to get the job done and close out games with clutch shots.

The Answer: Another nickname for Allen Iverson. The story goes that after Michael Jordan, people were always questioning who would be the next MJ. When Iverson entered the league, it was clear that he was "the answer."

Big Fundamental: An apt nickname was given to Tim Duncan due to, what else, his great fundamentals.

Big Shot Bob: Robert Horry's nickname was given to him due to his ability to make late-game shots under pressure, helping his teams sneak away with the victory.

Black Mamba: A self-given nickname by Kobe Bryant in reference to the 2003 film *Kill Bill* by Quentin Tarantino. It's a code name for a deadly assassin, the mentality Kobe would have, especially in late-game situations.

The Claw: Given to Kawhi Leonard in reference to his massive hands, This actually made him a great threat on defense.

The Dream: Hakeem Olajuwon's infamous nickname was given to him because of his fantastic footwork that put every player on the court to shame. Watching him move felt almost like a dream.

Diesel: One of Shaquille O' Neal's many nicknames. This one references how he has the strength and speed of a diesel engine.

Dr. J: Julius Erving's nickname due to how he operated on the court with "surgical proficiency."

Greek Freak: This nickname was given to a current legend in the making, Giannis Antetokounmpo. It reflects his Greek heritage and his freakish athleticism and frame that makes him nearly impossible to defend.

The Glove: The nickname for Gary Payton, a defensive legend who clamped down on his opponent like one would hold onto a baseball with a glove.

Jesus Shuttlesworth: The name of the character played by Ray Allen in the 1998 film *He Got Game*. The name was so iconic that it stuck with him throughout his career.

Jimmy Buckets: Sometimes, a nickname is perfect in its simplicity. This one is attributed to Jimmy Butler because of his ability to take and make shots, and in other words, he gets buckets.

Joker: The nickname was given to Nikola Jokic. It references not just his fun and whimsical playstyle, which is not usually seen by a center, but also his penchant for telling jokes, especially at press conferences.

The Mailman: Karl Malone's nickname. Why the mailman? Because he always delivered.

The Microwave: The nickname was given to Vinnie Johnson due to his ability to come off the bench and make shots in a short amount of time. In other words, he heated up quickly.

Pistol Pete: The nickname of legendary assist-maker Pete Maravich. The ball shot out of his hands with impressive speed and accuracy.

Round Mound of Rebound: A clever yet unusual nickname for Charles Barkley. On the one hand, it praised his amazing rebound skills. On the other hand, it also referenced his weight and body shape.

Timelord: A nickname that was born from Twitter. Robin Williams missed a few key appointments after being drafted. When the media chastised him for this, fans on Twitter poked fun at the outrage by saying he just operated on a different timeline and that he controls time and space.

Vinsanity: Definitely a contender for the greatest nickname of all time. Given to Vince Carter, it references his prime performances in the early 2000s, where his athleticism and powerful dunks felt like pure insanity to watch.

The Worm: A nickname that actually has nothing to do with basketball, and it belongs to Dennis Rodman, and apparently, it's in reference to the way he used to "wiggle around" while playing pinball as a kid.

Chapter 3: Top Ten Greatest Coaches

Arguably, there is no more challenging job in the NBA than being a head coach. You're faced with the unenviable task of taking a team full of players with different levels of experience, clashing egos, and varying attitudes and turning them into a juggernaut that will win the NBA championship. Preferably more than once. You have to study the strengths and weaknesses of your team, incorporate a play style everyone can get on board with, figure out lineups and rotations, and deal with the demands of the front office. And you're expected to do all these things in a set time frame, or else you're fired. All blame falls on your hands first, and all the praise comes to you last. It makes you wonder how these coaches manage to stay afloat in this league.

Well, the answer is they don't, at least for most of them. In fact, on some teams, coaches barely survive past one season. This lack of longevity is primarily due to two reasons. The first is the pressure, as mentioned earlier, to succeed. When you're the coach, all eyes fall on you to make all the pieces of the puzzle fit. You need to guide your players to victories and help them achieve their potential. If you can't do that, then the front office will find someone else. The second is that they're simply not a good fit for the team. Suppose the coach wants to put a new system in place but finds that the players are not accustomed to it, but the front office doesn't believe in it either. When the coach doesn't fit the environment of the team, it's easier to call it quits than to force something that isn't going to happen.

So when a coach is good, then they're *really* good. The greatest coaches of all time are the ones that have faced this pressure and thrived, going on to have long-tenured careers, they're the ones who implemented a system that worked to perfection (sometimes for more than one team), and they're the ones who players respect years after they're done playing for them. There have been many bad coaches and a good amount of okay coaches, but there are only a handful of truly great coaches. Here are ten of the greatest coaches of all time in no particular order.

Honorable Mentions: Erik Spoelstra, Steve Kerr, George Karl, Rick Carlisle

Number Ten: John Kundla

Throughout the decades of the NBA's existence, there have been many dynasties, many teams who have gone through years-long stretches of championship greatness. Still, there's one man who has the privilege of coaching the NBA's very first dynasty. That man is John Kundla. He took a team with multiple future Hall of Famers, saw their transition into the league, managed their existing attitudes and egos, and made the right calls on and off the court in order to achieve this feat. Just like Red Auerbach, John Kundla's coaching career started a couple of years before the great merger. In 1946, he was approached by the owners of a new professional basketball franchise in Minnesota called the Minneapolis Lakers to be their head coach.

He initially declined, but after they offered to double the salary he was making at his college head coach job, he accepted the job at the young age of thirty-one years old. They found immediate success after legendary player George Mikan joined the team, and they went on to win the 1948 NBL Championship. A year later, when the entire franchise jumped ship to the BAA, they won their league's championship, beating Red Auerbach and the Washington Capitols.

Kundla's effectiveness as a coach came as a result of his personality. He was a very mild-mannered person who rarely raised his voice; this allowed him to be highly observant and level-headed in the most stressful of situations. As a coach, he had this motto: "Praise loudly, blame softly." He earned the respect of his players, which is so important for any coach, which meant less clashing egos and more winning games. He won nearly sixty percent of his games across the NBL, BAA, and NBA and boasts an impressive playoff record of sixty wins and only thirty-five losses. When the NBA was officially born, Kundla established the league's first dynasty by leading the Lakers to five championships in the league's first six years of existence. Aside from George Mikan, he also had the privilege of coaching other Hall of Fame talents such as Jim Pollard, Vern Mikkelsen, Hot Rod Hundley, and Elgin Baylor. He was also chosen to coach the first four NBA All-Star Games. In 1960, when the Lakers were moving to Los Angeles, Kundla decided to stay in Minnesota, effectively ending his tenure as head coach of the team. Even so, he remained a Lakers fan for the rest of his life, and the Lakers honor him and his contributions to their early days by hanging his name from the rafters of their arena.

Number Nine: Jack Ramsay

If someone were to make a name for themselves twice in the NBA, they'd usually do so as a player and then later as a coach. Jack Ramsay took a different path; he cemented his legendary status in the NBA as a coach and a broadcaster. It's difficult to say which he was better at, he had a great mind for the game, and he proved that on the sidelines and in the booth. Regardless, he gave years of his life to the game in multiple capacities and deserved to be commemorated. "Dr. Jack" began his NBA coaching career for the Philadelphia 76ers in 1968. Ramsay's coaching style has two key components that would stay constant throughout his career. The first is an aggressive defense; he taught his teams to implement a zone press defense that had the players man a certain part of the court and disrupt the opposing team's ball handler. They effectively forced them to run the gauntlet before getting near the hoop when they got near them. The second is his emphasis on teamwork, players were allowed to shine and have breakout games, but in the end, no one was more important than the team. And no one was above criticism or praise. Ramsay's coaching style helped the 76ers become championship contenders and would later bring playoff success to the "bottom of the pile" Buffalo Braves. His most famous run as head coach would come with a move to Portland.

After hearing the Buffalo Braves' franchise was undergoing major changes (including a move to a new city), Ramsay decided that his time was done with the team. He took on the head coaching position for the Portland Trail Blazers, a team that was also near the bottom of the stands but was hoping to turn things around with this new coach and their young star Bill Walton. Ramsay orchestrated a dramatic turnaround for the team, and he led them to their first NBA championship in his very first year there. They would have made it back-to-back championships the next year, but Bill Walton injured his foot, and those dreams were dashed. Ramsay ended up coaching the Blazers for ten seasons, and though they only missed the playoffs once, they were never able to duplicate the championship success he had that very first year.

Nonetheless, he still remains the Blazers' most successful coach even to this day. After his coaching career ended, he found even more success as a broadcaster, using his great game knowledge and dynamic language to make him a household name for Miami Heat fans and anyone who tuned into ESPNRadio. He graced the ears of faithful listeners for years until the end of the 2012-2013 season. Two years later, in April 2014, Jack Ramsay would pass away due to complications regarding cancer. Even so, he continues to live on in the hearts of fans across the league who knew him as an excellent coach and broadcaster.

Number Eight: Lenny Wilkens

There have been some amazing players in the NBA that still have a hunger for the game after they retire, and so they make the seemingly logical transition to coaching. It makes sense in a way; they developed a great mind for the game when they were on the court, so it would make sense that they'd be just as effective on the sidelines. However, that's not always the case; most of the time, the best players often end up being the worst coaches. This is a phenomenon that isn't exclusive to basketball; for example, hockey legend Wayne Gretzky was a notoriously lousy coach who won less than half of his games. The likely reason for this is that these players operated at such an elite level that they didn't understand how the average player looked at the game. Their insane competitive edge meant they put much more pressure on their team than necessary. There are, however, exceptions to the rule. Sometimes, a great player develops the mindset needed to transition smoothly into a great coach. One such exception was Lenny Wilkens.

Lenny Wilkens began his NBA career in 1960 as a member of the St. Louis Hawks, though surprisingly, he wouldn't watch his first NBA game until *after* he was drafted. Wilkens had reservations about playing in the league, but after watching the Hawks' performance, he realized he could play so much better than the other guards on the team. When he committed to the game, it was clear that he was right. Wilkens played eight seasons with the Hawks as their starting point guard. He developed into an excellent playmaker, leading plays on the court and knowing exactly what to do if the play fell apart. After eight seasons with the Hawks, Wilkens was traded to the Seattle Sonics, and that's where he would get his first taste of the coaching experience. He was asked if he wanted to take on the role of "player-coach," meaning he would continue his regular player role as point guard for the team. He also had the added responsibilities of drawing up plays, setting lineups, and other coaching duties. He accepted the role, figuring he had nothing to lose. He'd be traded to the Cavaliers four seasons later, where he revitalized their entire offense. They developed actual plays and learned basic offensive maneuvers like the pick-and-roll that they could call on the fly if they needed to. After three seasons with the Cavaliers, Wilkens ended his playing career with the Portland Trail Blazers. Though he only played one season with them, it was an important one because he once again took on the role of player-coach. Having more experience with the role, Wilkens knew that he would need to focus more on the coach part rather than the player part if he was going to be successful at the job. At the end of the 1974-1975 season, he officially retired as an active player with nine All-Star game appearances, one All-Star Game MVP award, and the honor of being the league's leader in assists in 1970.

Wilkens made an immediate transition, shedding the term "player" from his title of player-coach. He learned much more about what it meant to be a coach while in Portland, and he decided to stay on after retiring to coach the team for one more season. That Blazers team ended the 1975-1976 season with a 37-45 record. With his time in Portland coming to an end, Wilkens took one season off before making his triumphant return to Seattle as the director of player personnel. However, with the Sonics facing a record of 5-17, Wilkens took on the job of head coach, and the team made a dramatic turnaround. This now dominant Sonics team made the Finals for two consecutive seasons, winning the championship the second time. Wilkens' coaching style was so successful because it mimicked his playing style. He was an incredibly unselfish playmaker, which translated well into a team-oriented brand of basketball. Wilkens coached a style where it mattered less about who took the shot and more about getting a teammate open. It was like he was a wizard, using his magic wand to turn a team lacking in star power into unstoppable juggernauts.

After eight more seasons coaching the Sonics (one of which he actually served as the team's general manager and vice president), Wilkens took his coaching skills back to Cleveland, where he once again worked his magic. He took a team full of young prospects and turned them from a losing team into playoff contenders. In the 1991-1992 season, the Cavaliers even made it all the way to the Eastern Conference Finals. Wilkens had a formula, a process, and he implemented it to great success wherever he went. When his time with the Cavaliers ended, he would circle his way back to the (now) Atlanta Hawks, where they would break franchise records and become the top team in their division. In 2000, when he was the coach for the Toronto Raptors, he would take them all the way to the Eastern Conference Semifinals. The magic didn't seem to run out until 2005 when he could only coach the New York Knicks to a 40-41 record, and he officially stepped down. However, despite that blemish, Wilkens' system resulted in wins for him and his teams. In 1995, after twenty-two seasons of coaching, his Hawks team beat the Washington Bullets, and in doing so, he gained his nine hundred and thirty-ninth win and became the winningest coach in NBA history. He'd end his coaching career with well over a thousand wins, and after all these years, he still ranks third in most regular-season wins by any coach.

Number Seven: Larry Brown

Larry Brown was the NBA's coach. This isn't just because of the long list of teams he's been the head coach of in the league but also because he's given so much to the game that his influence is still felt today. He is an example of a great student of the game who turned into one of its greatest teachers, every team he went to had great success, and that's no coincidence. He didn't have a set coaching style that he stubbornly implemented for every team he was involved with; he just knew exactly what every team needed to do in order to go from mediocre to a contender. The most effective teachers are keen to do that; they see the needs in each individual class and plan accordingly so that every student has a chance to succeed. Larry Brown continues to build his legacy to this day, but it first began in 1983.

Unlike many coaches on this list, Larry Brown was already an established name before he coached a single team in the NBA. He burst onto the scene due to his work with the University of Kansas, whom he built into a dynasty starting in 1983. Their former head coach had led them in back-to-back losing seasons, but that wouldn't be the case with Larry Brown at the helm. In his very first season with the team, the Jayhawks won the Big 8 Tournament and advanced to the NCAA tournament. They would make the tournament in all five seasons that Brown coached them. In 1987-1988, the Jayhawks went all the way and won the NCAA championship, and Larry Brown had officially formed that year's best team in college basketball. Throughout his time in Kansas, he won over seventy percent of his games, and he received Coach of the Year honors from the Big Eight Conference in 1986 and the NCAA in 1988. At the end of that historic 1988 season, Brown left college basketball temporarily and was hired by the San Antonio Spurs, beginning his influential run in the NBA.

His work does not exemplify Larry Brown's NBA career for one specific team; in fact, he never stayed on a team any longer than four seasons, it's memorable due to the way he "resurrected" multiple teams. He began working his magic with the Spurs, who he helped win their division twice, and from 1990-1991, they went from having their worst record in franchise history to their best. In 1992, he joined the Los Angeles Clippers and took them to the playoffs two times, the first time they'd done so since they were the Buffalo Braves. In 1993, he was hired by the Indiana Pacers, who he took to the Eastern Conference Finals twice in the four seasons he was there. Brown topped that with his run with the Philadelphia 76ers, who he took all the way to the NBA Finals in 2001. Perhaps his most tremendous success in the NBA came from his stint with the Detroit Pistons from 2003-2005. In the 2004 NBA Finals, Larry Brown and the Pistons infamously beat the Lakers star-studded superteam in five games to win the NBA Championship. In 2005, he notched his thousandth win as the coach of the New York Knicks. From 2008-2010 coached his ninth and final NBA team: the Charlotte Bobcats. Though they were young and lacked much experience, they saw significant improvement under his tutelage. In 2009, the Bobcats made it all the way to the playoffs, something they would only do twice while under the Bobcats name. Today, Brown has returned to college basketball and works as an assistant coach for the University of Memphis. He remains the only coach to have ever won an NCAA and NBA championship, and he also holds an NBA Coach of the Year award to add to his already impressive resume. With the mind for the game that he has, only time will tell if his head coaching days are truly behind him.

Number Six: Jerry Sloan

To last longer than one season as a head coach in the NBA is already a blessing. To make it all the way through to the end of your contract is impressive. But to last so long as head coach that you become so ingrained into the team's culture you're with is downright legendary. Such is the case for Jerry Sloan. This man spent more than half his life in the NBA, and he spent half his NBA life with one team: the Utah Jazz. But his contributions to the league didn't start there; they began when he was drafted fourth in the 1965 NBA Draft by the Baltimore Bullets. However, just a year later, the league added a new team named the Chicago Bulls, who chose Sloan during the expansion draft. His playing career would flourish in Chicago, where he would develop a tenacious style of defense, never giving up on a play and relentlessly guarding his opponent so they'd make a bad move and he could capitalize. He'd become part of the "Original Bulls," With his contributions, the team made the playoffs eight times in nine years and the Eastern Conference Finals twice. Persistent injuries ended up cutting Sloan's playing career short at just eleven seasons, but even within that time, he made it to two All-Star games, four All-NBA Defensive teams, and is still ranked in the top five for most points scored in Bulls franchise history.

Two years after retiring, Jerry Sloan returned to the Bulls first as a scout, then as an assistant coach, and then in 1979, he was promoted to head coach. Now leading them on the sidelines, Sloan posted a losing record after three seasons and one playoff appearance. The lackluster performance got him fired, but he remained relentless even as a coach. In 1985, Jerry Sloan officially began his tenure with the Utah Jazz as an assistant coach. He held this job for four seasons, and during the 1988-1989 season, the front office chose him to be the new head coach. It was a perfect fit. In this first era, Jerry Sloan had a promising team at his disposal led by two legendary players in John Stockton and Karl Malone. Sloan's no-nonsense style as a player translated well as a coach, players bought into the same idea, and the Utah Jazz became a defensive powerhouse and one of the best teams in the 90s. Who could ever forget the wars that Sloan and the Jazz fought against Michael Jordan and the Bulls in the NBA Finals? Though he never won a championship with this team, he still managed to take them to the playoffs for fifteen consecutive seasons, and he notched over ten seasons with fifty wins or more. This first era officially ended in 2003, when Stockton retired, and Malone joined the Lakers. Sloan and the Jazz lay dormant for three seasons, failing to make the playoffs, but their winning ways would eventually return, and Sloan-led basketball would start a second era.

He had a young team at his disposal with prospects such as Carlos Boozer, Andrei Kirilenko, and Deron Williams. People predicted that the Jazz would be one of the worst teams in the league. Still, they far exceeded their expectations posting a winning record their first year together, and in the 2006-2007 season, they made the playoffs and made it all the way to the Western Conference Finals. For the next four years, the Jazz remained legitimate championship contenders led by Boozer and Williams, who were now All-Stars, and during the 2008-2009 season, Sloan recorded his one-thousandth win.

In February 2011, Sloan resigned from his position and called it a career, citing a lack of energy for his departure. Though he never won a championship, he built a legend for himself that surpassed the need for one. It's rare for a coach to lead a team through more than one era, and it's rare for a coach to mold high-performing teams nearly every season of their career. Jerry Sloan achieved both, amassing more than one thousand and two hundred wins with almost a single team. Tragically, he died in 2020 from Parkinson's disease and dementia complications. But he remains a legend, not just for the Jazz but for the entire league.

Number Five: Red Auerbach

How different would Celtics history look if they'd never had Red Auerbach as a head coach? Thankfully, we never have to find out. Red Auerbach is another man synonymous with the team he coached; he is a Boston Celtics icon who led one of the team's very first dynasties. But his legacy doesn't start there; in fact, it begins before the NBA even existed. Red Auerbach first began coaching professional basketball in 1946 when he accepted the head coach job for the Washington Capitols in the BAA. He coached them for three seasons, in which he pioneered the "fast break," where his team would get the ball to one of their guards, who would streak down the court with the defense trailing behind him for an easy basket. Back then, teams played at a much slower pace, so this new offensive development greatly benefited Red's team. When the merger occurred and the BAA turned into the NBA, Red had moved on to coach the Tri-Cities Blackhawks, but he only stayed with them for one season due to disagreements with the owner. Meanwhile, over in Boston, the owner Walter Brown wanted to turn the Celtics' fortunes around and asked local sportswriters who they should hire as their head coach. The decision was unanimous: Red Auerbach.

He joined the team for the 1950-1951 season and went right to work, tasked with turning the team around. He implemented his fast break system, drafted players he believed fit the team's future success, and even broke the color barrier surrounding the league by drafting African-American Chuck Cooper. Red's methods turned the team into playoff contenders, but they couldn't put all the pieces together for those first six seasons to win a championship. And then, in the 1956 NBA Draft, the Celtics acquired legendary center Bill Russell, kickstarting the team's very first dynasty. Red built a more defensive-minded, teamwork-oriented team with an effective center to help anchor their defense. They forced their opponents to take tough shots, which resulted in (usually) Bill Russell grabbing the rebound and helping to kickstart the fast break. Finally, all the pieces fit together, and the Celtics found championship success. Not just once or twice, but through *many* seasons. From 1957-1966, the Celtics won nine NBA championships, eight of which were won through consecutive seasons. To this day, no team has even come close to winning eight championships in a row. When victory was close at hand, Red could be seen lighting up and smoking a cigar; he would go through *many* cigars during this dynasty. This run is how Red Auerbach's legacy truly started, but surprisingly his coaching career would end after the 1965-1966 season. He would, however, remain on the team as the General Manager and appointed Bill Russell as the Celtics' player-coach. Red continued to secure his legacy by reinforcing the team through shrewd trades and great draft selections throughout the years. Without him, the likes of Robert Parish, Larry Bird, and Kevin McHale may never have worn a Celtics jersey. He stayed on with the Celtics for decades, being involved with them in some capacity until he died in 2006. In 1967, the "Red Auerbach Trophy" was created to honor the recipient of the NBA's Coach of the Year award.

Number Four: Don Nelson

If the total number of wins was the sole metric to define the greatest coach of all time, then Don Nelson wins that honor easily. This man knew how to win, and he imprinted a winning mentality into every team he coached. Not only that, but he also made critical contributions to the league that still exist to this day. He had the motivation to succeed and was an innovator on the court and on the sidelines; without him, we might be watching a much different brand of basketball. Don Nelson's legendary NBA career began in 1962 when he was drafted seventeenth by the Chicago Zephyrs. After one season, he was picked up by the Los Angeles Lakers, where he played for two seasons and received some Finals experience when they lost to the St. Louis Hawks (who had a familiar face in Lenny Wilkens) and the Boston Celtics. Nelson found his best success when he joined the Celtics as a free agent in 1965. He averaged double digits in points and won multiple championships, even knocking down a famous clutch jumper in the 1969 NBA Finals that would help in securing the Celtics another championship. Nelson retired at the end of the 1975-1976 season, and after talking it over with his family, he started his coaching career with the Milwaukee Bucks.

Nelson took a lot of risks with this team, but in the end, they helped in creating his innovative coaching style. He was not afraid to trade assets to find players that better fit his team, and he experimented with having the small forwards direct the offense rather than the point guard (he'd call this variant of the position the "point forward"). He also experimented with a drastically different lineup, using the point forward to run the offense, having more effective shotmakers around the court, and putting the center at mid-court so that his opponent was away from the hoop. He called this method "Nellie Ball." Eleven seasons later, Nelson went to the Golden State Warriors, where he implemented a new system with them, a way of playing that emphasized high-speed basketball called the "run-and-gun" style. It called for a smaller lineup, so he picked out three guards and two forwards to bring the ball up the court as fast as possible and attempt a high volume of fast breaks. The Warriors made the playoffs four times in the six seasons he was there.

After coaching Team USA to a gold medal in the 1994 FIBA World Championship, and a year coaching for the New York Knicks, Nelson found more long-term employment with the Dallas Mavericks. In one of his first moves, he worked out trades on draft day that would put future legends Dirk Nowitzki and Steve Nash on his team with rising star Michael Finley. This trio and Nelson's brilliant coaching caused a massive turnaround for a Mavericks team that had been mediocre at best before this. Nelson led Dallas to playoff success during his eight seasons there, peaking in the 2002-2003 season when they won sixty games and nearly beat the Spurs in the Western Conference Finals. Nelson is also credited with coming up with the "Hack-a-Shaq" method, which is when players intentionally fouled the dominant big man Shaquille O' Neal to slow down his offensive momentum and force him to earn his points at the free-throw line. This method is still used today on centers with notoriously bad free-throw percentages. His final coaching stint came as a return to the Warriors in 2006. His coaching style helped improve the young team, which included players such as Monta Ellis, Stephen Jackson, and Baron Davis. In the 2007 playoffs, Nelson infamously took a Warriors team that just barely made it in as the eighth seed and went up against his old team, the Dallas Mavericks (who had won sixty-seven games this season). Six games later, the Warriors shocked the world by beating the Mavericks; it remains one of the biggest upsets in playoff history. Nelson's last couple of seasons with the Warriors ended with dreary losing seasons, and he resigned as head coach in September 2010. His last outstanding contribution to the team was pushing them to draft Stephen Curry in the 2009 NBA draft. Don Nelson's confidence and ability to innovate notched him win after win during his coaching career, and he contributed so many new styles of play to the game. As of now, he stands as the winningest coach in NBA history, recording 1,335 victories in the regular season alone.

Number Three: Pat Riley

Great coaches are able to create a dynasty from the team they're in charge of. So what does that make Pat Riley, who was able to do that with three teams? Pat Riley has one of the greatest minds for coaching that the league has ever seen. He thrived under pressure and carried an air of confidence with him that manifested in the players he worked with. He brought incredible levels of success to the Lakers, Knicks, and finally, the Heat, who he still works with to this day. The man with the fancy suits and slicked-back hair is no stranger to wins and certainly no stranger to championships, and his influence is still felt today. His legacy started with the Lakers; though he was just a role player on the court, he still shared in their success as they won a championship in 1972. After retiring in 1976, he continued on with the Lakers, but this time in a broadcasting role. In the 1981-1982 season, Pat Riley finally had his time to shine as he became the head coach for the team, working with legendary players Magic Johnson and Kareem Abdul-Jabbar. In just his first season as head coach, he led the team to an NBA championship, the first of many. He later dubbed this flashy, jaw-dropping version of the Lakers as "Showtime." And these Showtime Lakers went on to win three more championships in the 80s. After stepping down in 1990, Riley would continue his coaching career with the New York Knicks in 1991. Immediately, he showed his versatility as a coach by switching from the flashy, "showtime" playstyle to a more gritty, physical game that fit this Knicks team much better and made them easy playoff contenders. He found a formidable foe in the Jordan-led Chicago Bulls, and they met multiple times in the playoffs. Every time, however, Jordan and the Bulls would win; the only time Riley would beat the Bulls in the playoffs was when Jordan had temporarily retired.

Pat Riley ended his time with the Knicks in 1995, when he took a job as both the head coach and president of the Miami Heat. He would see this team through multiple eras of success and continue to do so long after relinquishing his head coaching duties. As a coach, he significantly improved the team and sent them to the playoffs multiple times in the 90s, and in 2006 he led them to the franchise's first NBA championship. As the president, he had a hand in orchestrating some of the most outstanding trades and acquisitions that have made the Heat a success many times over. These include acquiring Alonzo Mourning and Tim Hardaway in 1996, trading for the still impressive Shaquille O' Neal in 2006, landing both Chris Bosh and Lebron James in free agency in 2010, and putting together a team in 2020 that, while technically lacking a superstar, made it all the way to the NBA Finals as a fourth seed. Pat Riley ended his coaching career with three Coach of the Year awards, all with different teams, and though he hasn't coached a game since 2008, he still puts his great mind for the game to use to this day.

Number Two: Phil Jackson

The argument for Phil Jackson being the greatest coach of all time is pretty simple: he coached two of the NBA's most famous dynasties of all time. The name Phil Jackson holds a special place in the hearts of 1990s Bulls fans and 2000s Lakers fans for a very good reason. Without his contributions, they may have never achieved as much as they had. Phil Jackson is a man who knows exactly who he is, and that's displayed in his coaching style and unique personality. He's well-known for implementing the triangle offense- developed during his early coaching days by fellow assistant coach Tex Winters- which involved constant ball movement and coordination between everyone on the court. And he emphasized the importance of defense and the players staying on their man to pressure them into making a bad play or shot. His personality made him stand out in the league. As a result of his upbringing, mindful attitude, and fascination with Eastern philosophies, he would be dubbed "The Zenmaster." A fitting nickname if there ever was one, in a league full of loud and hot-headed coaches, Phil stood out for always remaining calm even under the most stressful of circumstances such as leading two separate teams through two separate "three-peats" with the NBA championship.

Despite spending years as a key role player on the New York Knicks, Phil Jackson almost never became a coach in the NBA. While honing his coaching skills outside the league, he kept applying for coaching positions in the NBA but was constantly turned down. It wasn't until 1987 that Phil got his first opportunity as an assistant coach with the Chicago Bulls, and now his legacy could truly begin. In 1989, he took on the head coach role and emulated the lessons he learned as an assistant. He implemented a team-oriented playstyle reinforced by the triangle offense. Phil consistently had the team's best interests at heart and meditated on the choices he needed to make in order for them to succeed. And success came through the perfect storm of Phil's coaching and a star-studded team led by Michael Jordan, including Scottie Pippen, Horace Grant, Steve Kerr, and Dennis Rodman. This dynasty won six championships throughout the 1990s. Due to rising tensions with the Bulls general manager Jerry Krause, Phil left the team at the end of the 1997-1998 season and took a year-long sabbatical.

In 1999, he decided to give coaching one more chance, this time signing with the Lakers. He was once again graced with a team full of superstars and future Hall of Famers such as Kobe Bryant, Shaquille O' Neal, Derek Fisher, Robert Horry, and Brian Shaw. In his first three years coaching the team, the Lakers dominated the league and went on to "three-peat" with the championship just as the Bulls did a few years prior. Phil's approach to the game never wavered. He drilled the triangle offense into the Laker culture and did his best to mediate the clashing egos and meditate with the team. Meditation was an essential part of the game prep for Phil. Just like with the Bulls, he had the Lakers meditate before every game. The calmness and mindfulness that came from it helped steer the Lakers to that first great dynasty. More front office drama pushed Phil out of coaching after the 2003-2004 season, but he returned in 2005. After a few tumultuous years, Phil Jackson and the Lakers found more championship success from 2009-2011. After the 2010-2011 season, Phil put his health first and officially retired from coaching. Even so, his popularity with the Lakers fans remained, and when the team was looking to hire a new head coach in 2013, fans clamored for Phil to come back. He didn't, subsequently ensuring he ended his coaching career on top.

Number One: Gregg Popovich

We end our list with arguably the greatest active head coach in the league, someone who has seen his fair share of dynasties and who has deeply ingrained himself into his team's culture. One could argue that Gregg Popovich isn't just the head coach of the Spurs; Gregg Popovich is the San Antonio Spurs. Generations of players have come and gone, generations of fans have watched the game evolve, and through it all, Gregg has become one of the league's greatest constants. His career started and will most likely end in San Antonio. After six years as an assistant coach, he took on the head coach position for the team in the middle of the 1996-1997 season. He got off to a rocky start at first, and by the end of the season, he recorded seventeen wins and forty-seven losses. This kind of losing season would never happen again under Gregg Popovich's watch. In fact, for the next twenty-two seasons, the Spurs would never win less than forty games. The only blemish was the lockout season in 1999, where they won thirty-seven out of their fifty games played, though that same season also ended with the Spurs holding the championship high.

Gregg Popovich is a winning coach, he and the Spurs have been synonymous with winning for nearly three decades now, and that has to do with the players and their style of play. Gregg has had the privilege of coaching some of the most incredible talents in NBA history, such as David Robinson, Tim Duncan, Tony Parker, Manu Ginobli, and Kawhi Leonard, and it's arguable whether or not they would have become such great players if they weren't playing under Pop's system. He has always had a knack for seeing the full potential of a player and helping them to reach it, rarely has there ever been "lost causes" on the Spurs because Gregg believes in everyone on his team and brings out the best in them. It's akin to the "chicken or egg" scenario: Are the players great because of what Pop brings out of them? Or does Pop choose players he already sees greatness in? Regardless of the answer, the results speak for themselves. Gregg Popovich has led the Spurs to five NBA championships and counting during his nearly thirty-year run as head coach. His teams have fearlessly faced off against the "three-peat" Lakers, their in-state rivals the Dallas Mavericks, the Miami Heat super team, and the flashy game-changing Golden State Warriors. The Spurs have finally slowed down in recent years and are now at the closest they've ever been to a rebuilding phase. But it only feels like a matter of time that Pop assembles the team he needs once more to get the Spurs back to their winning ways. Gregg Popovich holds three Coach of the Year awards and holds the great distinction of being the winningest coach in NBA history.

Chapter 4: Top Ten Teams in NBA History

Basketball is, and always will be, a team sport. Its origins emphasized the importance of teamwork, and more often than not, you'll find NBA fans more loyal to a team than any specific player. There's just something about the image of the greatest athletes in the world suiting up together with the common goal of winning that makes the sport so memorable and exciting to watch. There are currently thirty teams in the NBA, and throughout history, there have been iterations of these teams that rank well above the rest. Whether it's their innate ability to win, the star power throughout the roster, the championships they brought to their city, or how they changed the game, these ten teams will live on through history as the greatest to ever grace the hardwood.

Honorable Mentions: The 2010-2011 "Grit and Grind" Memphis Grizzlies, the 1971-1972 Los Angeles Lakers, the 2003-2004 Detroit Pistons, the 2013-2014 "Lob City" Los Angeles Clippers

Number Ten: 1966-1967 Philadelphia 76ers

The oldest team on this list! But still a team worth talking about due to their extended period of dominance during this season. In an Eastern Conference ruled by Bill Russel and the Celtics, you had the 76ers, who were just as impressive but just needed to put all the pieces together. In the 1966-1967 season, they finally did it. They'd built a roster full of the greatest scorers in the league. Any one of them could have a fantastic game where they'd shoot the lights out. You had future Hall of Famers in Hal Greer, Chet Walker, and Billy Cunningham, who all averaged around twenty points per game, Wali Jones, who would be an essential contributor in the playoffs, and the legend himself, Wilt Chamberlain. A giant among men in both the literal and figurative sense, Wilt Chamberlain, was a man who played the game to such perfection that they had to change the rules in order to make things fair for the other teams. He was a scoring machine, a defensive monster, and if there weren't recorded accounts of him playing in the league, you would believe he was a myth. They called him, among other things, Mr. 100 due to the fact that he once scored one hundred points in a single game, the most scored by anyone in NBA history. In this season alone, he was averaging twenty-four points (which was a low for him), twenty-four rebounds, and eight assists. With all these pieces in place, the Sixers tore through the regular season, going 46-4 in their first fifty games (the most incredible start to a season in NBA history) and ending the season with a 68-13 record. In the first round of the playoffs, they beat the Cincinnati Royals in five games and did so in the next round against Bill Russel and the Celtics. In a series that should have been more competitive, Wilt was a man on a mission, and he set the pace for the series, averaging twenty-one points and thirty-two rebounds in the five games it took to dismantle the Celtics. The San Francisco Warriors put up a bit more fight in the Finals by winning two games, but the Sixers would not be denied and took the series in six games. They started the season strong and ended it even stronger, and this run of dominance cements them as one of the greatest teams of all time.

Number Nine: 2013-2014 San Antonio Spurs

From 1997 to 2017, the San Antonio Spurs remained a team you would always have to look for in your rearview mirror. They posted winning season after winning season, and more often than not, they were championship contenders. And in the tough Western Conference, their consistent winning ways are an accomplishment in and of itself. The greatest iteration of this Spurs team came in the 2013-2014 season when perfect coaching aligned with the ideal roster. The year before saw this team losing in six games to the Miami Heat (see above), and with a strong motivation to seek revenge, Gregg Popovich assembled the team he needed to do just that. A prime Tim Duncan continued to lead the team. With him were the always reliable veteran guards Tony Parker and Manu Ginobli, sharpshooter Danny Green, international gems Patty Mills and Tiago Splitter, and the rising star Kawhi Leonard. Pop brought out the best in all his players, and their best gave them a 62-20 record at the end of the regular season. They found themselves in the familiar land of the playoffs, first facing off against a familiar foe in the Dallas Mavericks. Surprisingly, the eighth-seeded Mavericks were able to push the Spurs to seven games with narrow margins of victory, but in the end, the Spurs came up on top. In the next round, they beat the Blazers in five games and would end up meeting the young and hungry Thunder in the conference finals. Both teams wanted another chance at the heat, but it would be the Spurs getting the honor of a rematch at the end of six games. Though the Miami Heat super team was still mostly intact, a rejuvenated Spurs team went into the Finals ready to redeem themselves. This series wasn't as close as last year's, and it only took five games to beat the Heat (who would never be the same after this series). The Spurs were the new NBA champions, Tim Duncan had received his fifth title, and Kawhi Leonard was voted the Finals MVP.

Number Eight: 2007-2008 Boston Celtics

Sometimes, the best teams are formed by the best of circumstances. All the dice seemed to fall the Celtics way before the 2007-2008 season as they were able to seamlessly create one of the first superteams of the modern era. During the 2007 NBA Draft, the Boston Celtics orchestrated a trade that would send a second-round pick, Wally Szczerbiak, Delonte West, and Jeff Green for center Glen Davis and three-point sharpshooter Ray Allen. A month later, they would take a big gamble by trading seemingly half their bench and two first-round picks for Timberwolves star Kevin Garnett. That gamble would end up paying off. The Celtics had paired their All-Star small forward Paul Pierce with one of the league's greatest shooters in Ray Allen and the best power forward in the league Kevin Garnett to create "The Big Three," a term that would be used throughout the years to describe three star-caliber players coming together on one team. While they now had a team full of effective scorers, their defense made this Celtics team so great. They didn't need to put up big numbers every night because their defense ensured the opposing team couldn't get anything past them; it was rare for them to get anywhere near a hundred points against the Celtics. This was especially true when Kevin

Garnett played; the other team's field goal percentage plummeted when he was on the floor. In the year before, the Celtics finished with the second-worst record in the league at 24-58. This year, in a dramatic turnaround, they went 66-16 and had the best regular-season record in the league. Despite being the number one seed, they faced a tough road in the playoffs. How tough? The eighth-seeded Hawks pushed them all the way to seven games. Still, they persevered and made it to the second round, where they'd face a Cavaliers team led by a young and determined Lebron James. After being pushed to another seven games, the Celtics finally beat the Cavaliers and advanced to the Eastern Conference Finals, where they faced another defensive-oriented team in the Detroit Pistons. Six grueling games later, the Celtics came out victorious and would head to the NBA Finals to face their eternal rivals, the Los Angeles Lakers. The first four games were close, back-and-forth affairs, but they still managed to go up 3-1. Kobe and the Lakers stepped it up in game five to breathe more life into this series, but the undeniable Celtics would close things out in game six. The gamble paid off in the best way possible, the Boston Celtics were champions for the first time in twenty-two years, and at the end of it all, Kevin Garnett joyously exclaimed, "Anything is possible!"

Number Seven: 2012-2013 Miami Heat

Few teams are lucky to say that they had one of the greatest players of all time in their prime, and that's exactly what the Miami Heat had with Lebron James. The 2011-2014 iteration of the Miami Heat might arguably be the most hated team since the Bad Boy Pistons nearly three decades ago. And it wasn't because they played the same physical style of basketball, but because their roster was insanely good from top to bottom. They had Heat legend Dwyane Wade, one of the best power forwards in the game Chris Bosh, defensive big men Chris Andersen and Juwan Howard, veteran sharpshooters like Ray Allen, Mike Miller, and Shane Battier, and of course Lebron James, a man who was just now entering his prime. They were a force on offense and defense, coached by another Heat legend in Erik Spoelstra. This was during a time when the league had several championship contenders, and yet it was the Miami Heat who were entering the 2012-2013 season as the reigning champions. With such a big target on their backs, every single victory felt like a battle, and just when the opposing team thought they had the champions on the ropes, they would always find a way to bounce back. Their winning ways allowed them to go on a twenty-seven-game winning streak during the regular season, the third-highest win streak in NBA history. This was a heavily-covered stretch of basketball. Every team wanted to be the one to finally beat the streak (the Chicago Bulls would eventually do so). Thanks to that streak, and a regular-season full of top-level basketball, the Heat would end the season with a 66-16 record and a ticket to the playoffs. They made quick work of the Bucks in the first round and lost only one game to the Bulls in the second round before beating them too. In the Eastern Conference Finals, they faced a formidable rival in the Indiana Pacers, who *did* play a physical and defensive-oriented game. The Pacers pushed the defending champions to seven games before a prime Lebron took care of business (racking up thirty-two points in game seven) to take the Heat to the NBA Finals once more. There they would face another great challenge in the Spurs, who had never lost a Finals series up to this point. The teams went blow-for-blow every game until game six when the fortunes seemed to be in the Spurs' favor. This story might have a different ending if it wasn't for Ray Allen's game-tying three with seconds to go in the fourth quarter. As it stands, the Heat capitalized in overtime in game six and took care of business in game seven to hand the Spurs their first loss in the Finals. The Miami Heat superteam were the NBA champions for the second season in a row.

Number Six: 1988-1989 Detroit Pistons

If you want proof that basketball is as physical a sport as any others, you need to look no further than the 1988-1989 Detroit Pistons. This team was the definition of a "defensive powerhouse," bothering opponents left and right with their intense pressure and suffocating coverage. They made you earn your baskets. But their physical brand of basketball made them one of the most hated teams in the league, earning them the nickname of the "Bad Boys," In today's league, where physical play results in a foul more often than not, this team might not have been as dominant. But they thrived in the 80s, and they deserve a look back to see what made them so great. The Bad Boy Pistons have the accolade of being the toughest match-up Michael Jordan had to face. Before he and the Bulls could run the 90s, they had to run the gauntlet of a team that included Bill Laimbeer, Joe Dumars, Isiah Thomas, and a prime Dennis Rodman. Dominant big men and elite perimeter defenders meant they could bother any opponent anywhere on the court. And they were just as big of a threat on offense too. Thomas could outpace defenders to get to the hoop, Dumars could shoot from the perimeter, and Laimbeer had a great three-point shot. This team lacked all-stars, and yet all their players were stars in their own right which is how they entered the playoffs that year with a 63-19 record. Their dominance continued by sweeping Larry Bird and the Celtics, then doing the same to the Milwaukee Bucks in the second round. In the Eastern Conference Finals, they faced their toughest fight in the Bulls, who were able to win two games before they too were taken down by the Bad Boys. In the NBA Finals, they met up with Magic Johnson and the Lakers and, just as they had done up to that point, played the game their way. Four games later, they were crowned the champions of the league.

Number Five: 1985-1986 Boston Celtics

The NBA in the 80s was headlined by one of the sports' greatest rivalries, and on one side of that rivalry, you had the Boston Celtics. In the 1985-1986 season, they had assembled a roster riddled with future Hall of Famers such as Larry Bird, Robert Parish, Kevin McHale, Danny Ainge, and Bill Walton. All these players were at or near their prime, and any one of them could have been the star player on their own team, but instead, they all came together to fight for multiple championships. Everyone on this team could play; everyone on this team could shoot. If you put the ball in anyone's hands, they would most likely convert it into a bucket. They had players who could drive into the paint, players that were a threat on the perimeter, and players that could hit from deep. If you were the opposing team and weren't guarding your man at all times, they would make you pay for that mistake with an easy bucket. They were a force to be reckoned with, boasting a 67-15 record at the end of the season with only *one loss* at home. In the playoffs, they were met in the first round by Michael Jordan and the Bulls, who they subsequently swept, and in the second round, they lost one game to the Hawks before putting them away as well. Another sweep in the next round against the Bucks ensured a date in the Finals against Hakeem Olajuwon and the Rockets. Impressively, the Rockets would push them to six games, but they were eventually beaten as well. The Celtics would win more championships in the 80s, but this was the peak of their dominance.

Number Four: 1986-1987 Los Angeles Lakers

On the other side of that 80s rivalry, you had the Lakers, who had assembled a star-studded team of their own. By 1986, they had a roster led by Magic Johnson, an aging yet still dominant center Kareem Abdul-Jabbar, offensive machines Byron Scott and James Worthy, and fantastic role players A.C. Green, Kurt Rambis, and Michael Cooper. They had been dubbed the "Showtime" Lakers during this run because of their exciting, entertaining style of play consisting of constant fast breaks, flashy moves, and high-scoring games. Led by coach Pat Riley, the team had its best run during the 1986-1987 season, one year removed from a heartbreaking loss in the Western Conference Finals to the Rockets. Looking to redeem themselves, the team took everything that made them great and worked to be even better. They held the number one offense in the league led by Magic Johnson, who would have an MVP-caliber year, seven players on their team averaged double digits in scoring, and they would constantly blow out their opponents. Heading easily into the playoffs with a 65-17 record, the Lakers had all the momentum in the world. Their first-round matchup against the Nuggets wasn't even close, and in the second round, they only lost one game to the Warriors before closing them out in five games. In the Western Conference Finals, they faced another formidable team in the Sonics, and they ended up sweeping them too in order to set up another confrontation with the Celtics. Like all their battles, this one was intense and physical. Had Magic Johnson missed his skyhook at the end of game four, all hope may have been lost for the Lakers. But magic made the shot, honoring his long-time teammate Kareem, and the team would eventually defeat the Celtics in six games. The Showtime Lakers were on top of the world again, and Magic Johnson received both regular-season MVP and Finals MVP honors.

Number Three: 2000-2001 Los Angeles Lakers

In a time when NBA fans were cooling down from watching the Chicago Bulls dominate the league for most of the 90s, another dynasty was quickly building in California. From 1999-2002, the Los Angeles Lakers boasted an unstoppable and entertaining brand of play akin to their Showtime days, resulting in a three-peat with the NBA Championships. The best version of this team is the one that ran it back after winning their first championship. The team was led by a prime Shaquille O' Neal and rising All-Star Kobe Bryant, with a tremendous supporting cast such as veterans Brian Shaw and Horace Grant, reliable point guard Derek Fisher, and clutch shooter Robert Horry. And guiding them through this three-peat was the legendary coach Phil Jackson. Truth be told, this team felt like it had eased off the gas a little bit, as evident by the fact that they only won fifty-six games (eleven less than the year before), but they're not on this list because of their regular-season run. They're here because of their legendary playoff run when they pressed their foot on the gas and never looked back. Shaq was still the de facto leader during this run and set the pace for their dominance, averaging thirty points and fifteen rebounds through the playoffs. But Kobe was emerging as a threat of his own, averaging twenty-nine points and six assists. With their performances, they would end up sweeping their entire bracket. First, they made quick work of the Blazers, then they did the same with the Kings, and then they faced the best team in the West, their greatest threat to repeat, the Spurs. The Lakers also swept them. In the 2001 Finals, they met Allen Iverson and the 76ers. Game one saw A.I. go off for forty-eight points to shock the world and prove the Lakers were mortal. But that was the only shot they would land on the reigning champions, and the Lakers would go on to win the next four games and hoist the trophy up with an overall historical record of 16-1 in the playoffs. The Kobe-Shaq duo proved themselves to be the most incredible duo in the league and maybe even all of the sports, and that playoff record would remain unmatched for sixteen years.

Number Two: 1995-1996 Chicago Bulls

Last but certainly not least, we have the team that defined 90s basketball and cemented Michael Jordan, who had come out of retirement, as one of the greatest players of all time. The 1995-1996 Bulls are widely considered to be the peak of their dominance against the rest of the league. It didn't feel like East vs. West during this time. It felt like the NBA vs. the Chicago Bulls, every team wanted to be the one to dethrone the reigning champions, and several teams could undoubtedly do it. You had the Utah Jazz led by Stockton and Malone, the Seattle Sonics, who were the best team in the West, the Orlando Magic with its talented center Shaquille O' Neal, the Barkley-led Phoenix Suns, and of course, the reigning champions, the Houston Rockets. But with Michael Jordan being persuaded to come out of his first retirement, no one would stand in the way of him and the Chicago Bulls. Including Jordan, their roster consisted of a prime Scottie Pippen, defensive big man Dennis Rodman, three-point machine Steve Kerr, a rising star in Toni Kukoc, and of course their ever-reliable coach Phil Jackson. With a team full of superstars in their prime and an enviously good bench, the Bulls went on to dominate the regular season. They would go on to have the highest offensive *and* defensive rating in the entire league, and they would post their historical 72-10 record (which would stand for twenty years).

The Bulls carried their dominance straight into the playoffs. They easily took care of the Heat in the first round, with their victories being blowouts. They faced off against Patrick Ewing and the Knicks in the second round, but they too were no match for the determined Bulls, and they lost the series in five games. In the Eastern Conference Finals, they again squared off with the Orlando Magic, who had beaten them the prior year. This time, the tale would be different, and the Bulls swept the magic en route to another NBA Finals. Their opponent, their last obstacle, was the Seattle Sonics. The Bulls got off to a hot start, winning the first three games, but the Sonics weren't going to go down so easily, and they took games four and five. This was going to be a fight. In a grueling game six, the Bulls pulled out all the stops. Michael Jordan scored twenty-two points, Pippen followed close behind with seventeen, and Dennis Rodman cleaned up on defense with nineteen rebounds. With their three best players performing at the level that brought them that 72-10 record, the Bulls finally defeated the Sonics, and they capped off their historic season with the NBA championship. This would be the start of the Bulls' second three-peat and arguably the most infamous run of Michael Jordan's career. The Bulls achieved a level of success this year that has only been matched once in history, and time will tell if there will ever be another team like this.

Number One: 2016-2017 Golden State Warriors

The rise of the Golden State Warriors in the late 2010s seemingly came out of nowhere. One minute, this California-based team with an injury-prone point guard was planted near the bottom of their conference, and the next, they were perched at the very top of the league. It didn't happen out of nowhere; obviously, the Warriors' rise came from smart draft choices, Steph Curry coming into his own as the league's unanimously best shooter, and finally, an effective coaching change in the 2014-2015 season from Mark Jackson to Steve Kerr. With all the pieces in place, they went on a phenomenal five-year run as the best team in the Western Conference, winning three championships along the way and, in 2016, achieving the best regular-season record in NBA history of seventy-three wins and just *nine losses*. This golden dynasty reached its peak during the 2016-2017 season when Kevin Durant, one of the best players in the league today, joined the team in free agency. An already stacked team that included Steph Curry, Klay Thompson, Draymond Green, and veteran Andre Iguodala were now adding a former MVP to their rotation. In fact, when all five of these players were on the court at the same time, they were known as the "Death Lineup." They were an unstoppable force, easily coasting through the regular season with a 67-15 record. This team had multiple scoring threats, elite defenders, and an all-time great coach; all these things came together as a perfect storm entering the playoffs. They swept every single one of their opponents in their bracket to become Western Conference Champions and set up a rematch with last year's champions, the Cleveland Cavaliers. Unlike that year, this series wasn't even close, and they only lost one game before running right through the Cavaliers to win the franchise's fifth championship and right their wrong from last year's series.

Chapter 5: NBA Trivia and Forgotten Facts

The NBA has a history that spans almost an entire century, so it's natural that some parts of that history have fallen through the cracks. In this chapter, we're going to dig up some more of that history to find the wildest, most interesting facts from a league that's seen some fantastic and exciting things.

Did You Know…?

- the shot clock was introduced to the NBA in 1954 and was invented by Danny Biasone.
- the three-point line wasn't introduced to the NBA until 1979.
- Earl Lloyd is the first black person to play in an NBA game.
- the first non-white player to play in the NBA was a Japanese-American named Wataru Misaka, who debuted in the 1947-1948 season.
- the NBA logo is a silhouette of legendary point guard Jerry West.
- the first NBA All-Star Game was played in 1951.
- only four players have ever recorded a quadruple-double:

Nate Thurmond, Alvin Robertson, Hakeem Olajuwon, and David Robinson.

- the bird on the Twitter logo is named Larry the Bird in homage to Celtics legend Larry Bird.
- the tallest player in NBA history is Manute Bol at 7'7."
- the shortest player in NBA history is Mugsy Bogues at 5'.3" Despite this, he recorded thirty-nine blocks during his career.
- Kobe Bryant's middle name was "Bean."
- Ray Allen's first name is actually "Walter."
- Ron Artest changed his name before the 2011-2012 season to Metta World-Peace.
- Russell Westbrook once averaged a triple-double for an entire season.
- The largest margin of victory in league history came in 2021 when the Grizzlies beat the Thunder 152-79, meaning they won by seventy-three points.
- the highest-scoring game occurred in 1983. It was a triple-overtime game between the Denver Nuggets and the Detroit Pistons. The Pistons won with a final score of 186-184.
- the longest game in NBA history occurred in 1951 between the Indianapolis Olympians and the Rochester Royals. The game went to six overtimes, and the Olympians won with a final score of 75-73.
- though Michael Jordan has infamously worn the number 23 throughout his career, there was a short period of time after ending his first retirement that he wore the number 45.

- the only franchises that have never moved from their home cities are the Boston Celtics and New York Knicks.
- the Washington Wizards have undergone five name changes. They went from the Chicago Packers to the Chicago Zephyrs to the Baltimore Bullets to the Capital Bullets to the Washington Bullets before finally settling on the Washington Wizards in 1997.
- the best regular-season record belongs to the 2015-2016 Golden State Warriors, who went 73-9.
- the worst regular-season record belongs to the 2011-2012 Bobcats, who went 7-59.
- Shaquille O' Neal broke two NBA backboards from dunking the ball too hard.
- star power forward Pau Gasol went to medical school before joining the NBA.
- the full name of the Knicks is the New York Knickerbockers.
- the youngest person to ever play in the NBA was Andrew Bynum; he made his debut in the league when he was eighteen years and six days old.
- the longest NBA career belongs to Vince Carter, who played for twenty-two seasons in the league before retiring after the 2019-2020 season.
- Michael Jordan has the worst result in the Three-Point Shooting Contest, only scoring five points.
- despite being one of the top five scorers in NBA history, Kobe Bryant also holds the record for the most missed shots at 14,481.
- the biggest comeback went to the Utah Jazz in 1996. They

overcame a thirty-six-point deficit against the Denver Nuggets to win the game 107-103.

- Trevor Ariza has been traded to twelve different teams in his career, the most in NBA history.
- the Lakers and Celtics are tied for the franchise with the most championships in the league at seventeen.
- Bill Russell won eleven NBA championships, the most of any player in his career.
- Jason Kidd holds the record for the most turnovers in a single game at fourteen.
- Kareem Abdul-Jabbar holds the record for the most points in NBA history at 38,387.
- John Stockton holds the record for most assists in NBA history at 15,806. He also holds the record for most steals at 3,265.
- Wilt Chamberlain holds the record for most rebounds in NBA history at 23,924.
- Hakeem Olajuwon holds the record for most blocks in NBA history at 3,830.
- Stephen Curry is the only person to be unanimously voted regular-season MVP, which he won during the 2015-2016 season.
- Lebron James has played more playoff games than half the teams in the league. He is also the first player to win the Finals MVP award with three different teams (Cavaliers, Heat, Lakers).
- there are currently eleven teams that have never won an NBA championship: the Timberwolves, Clippers, Nuggets, Pacers, Hornets, Nets, Grizzlies, Jazz, Suns, Pelicans,

and Magic.

- during a one-week span in March 2007, Kobe Bryant scored at least fifty points in four consecutive games.

- Bobby Jones played for five different teams in the 2007-2008 season. They were the Nuggets, Grizzlies, Rockets, Heat, and Spurs.

- Michael Jordan holds the record for most points scored in a playoff game at sixty-three.

- in 1961, Wilt Chamberlain scored seventy-eight points and grabbed forty-three rebounds in one game.

- Rasheed Wallace holds the record for most technical fouls at 304. He also holds the record for most ejections at twenty-nine, one of which he received by simply staring at the referee.

- Nikola Jokic holds the record for the fastest amount of time to get a triple-double at fourteen minutes and thirty-three seconds.

- before getting drafted, Lakers legend Kobe Bryant had a workout and interview with the Celtics.

- despite being only 5'6", Spud Webb won the 1986 Slam Dunk Contest.

- Nate Robinson, also a short player, has won three Slam Dunk contests, the most out of anyone. He won in 2006, 2009, and 2010.

- Air Jordans used to be against the NBA dress code. Nike would pay a fine so that Michael Jordan could wear a pair for his games.

- Dennis Rodman once illegally married himself.

- Ron Artest applied to Circuit City during his rookie year to get their employee discount.
- Shaquille O' Neal has only made one three-pointer in his career. Meaning he's broken more backboards than he's made threes.
- Vince Carter once dunked over a seven-foot-two player during the 2000 Olympics.
- the most expensive basketball card is an autographed Steph Curry rookie card which sold for nearly six million dollars in 2021.

The Forgotten Facts

1. The NBA was in a huge financial crisis during its early days. In order for the league to stay afloat, they relied on the financial backing of Fred Zollner, who, at the time, was the owner of the Fort Wayne Pistons.
2. The Chicago Bulls were the first expansion team in NBA history, joining the league in 1966.
3. Before Magic Johnson and Larry Bird were part of the great Lakers-Celtics rivalry of the 80s, they first played against each other in college. It was a 1979 NCAA tournament game between Michigan State (Magic's school) and Indiana State (Bird's school).
4. The small state of Rhode Island used to have an NBA team back in 1946, and they were called the Providence Steamrollers and only lasted three seasons.
5. Jump balls used to happen after every made basket.
6. When great financial disagreements are occurring in the league (i.e. wage disparity, contract disputes, the strain between large market and small market teams), they will

sometimes go into a lockout until the disagreements have been settled, sometimes resulting in a shortened season. There have been four NBA lockouts to date (1995, 1996, 1998, 2011). 1998 was the most prolonged lockout, and it lasted for over six months.

7. In an eerie instance of fate, Pete Maravich once told a newspaper that he didn't want to play in the NBA for ten years and die of a heart attack at the age of forty. After concluding a ten-year career in the league, he died of a heart attack at forty years old.

8. After Lebron James went into free agency in 2010, he decided to broadcast him choosing which team to go to for the next season on ESPN. The televised special was called "The Decision."

9. Since 1979, every NBA champion based in the Western Conference has come from either Texas or California. These are the Houston Rockets, San Antonio Spurs, Dallas Mavericks, Los Angeles Lakers, and the Golden State Warriors.

10. Jerry West is the only player to win Finals MVP despite being on the losing team. In the 1969 Finals, the Celtics beat the Lakers, but West's performance in the series was too incredible not to commemorate. He averaged thirty-eight points, seven assists, and five rebounds per game.

11. In 2000, Paul Pierce was stabbed in a nightclub eleven times in the face, neck, and back, yet he returned to the court three days later and started all eighty-two games that season.

12. In the 90s, the Dunk Contest was getting so bad that the league canceled it after the 1997 contest, and it would not

come back until the 2000 All-Star Weekend. The 2000 Dunk Contest is considered one of the greatest of all time, thanks to an electric performance by Vince Carter.

13. The 2000 NBA Draft class is widely considered to be the worst of all time. Only nine players drafted that year averaged more than ten points in their entire career. Its biggest standouts were Michael Redd, who made the All-NBA Third team in 2004, and Kenyon Martin, who played one All-Star game.

14. Inversely, the 1984 NBA Draft class is arguably the best in history. Some of the most famous players in the game were drafted this year, including assist-leader John Stockton, Charles Barkley, Hakeem "The Dream" Olajuwon, and of course, Michael Jordan.

15. In March 2017, Phoenix Suns shooting guard Devin Booker decided to go off against the Celtics and score seventy points in a random regular-season game. This is the tenth most points scored in a regular-season game, and at just twenty years of age, it makes him the youngest player ever to score more than sixty points in a game. Yet despite his stellar performance, the Suns ended up losing the game.

16. The NBA has gone to great efforts to make the league an international sensation one way they've done this is by scheduling exhibition games to be played outside the United States. Israel held the first overseas game in 1978, where the Washington Bullets lost to the Maccabi Tel Aviv. The first regular-season game to be played overseas was in 1990 in Tokyo between the Jazz and Suns. Since then, the NBA has played games in places like Germany, the Philippines, France, the Bahamas, and Mexico City.

The last international game occurred in January 2020 in Paris, where the Bucks beat the Hornets.

17. The largest trade in NBA history occurred on August 2, 2005, that saw thirteen players traded amongst five teams: the Heat, Grizzlies, Jazz, Hornets, and Celtics.

Chapter 6: Inspiring Stories

The NBA is full of exciting action and jaw-dropping performances, but it's also home to some of the most inspiring stories. Though we may consider these athletes to be successful, larger-than-life figures, that hasn't always been the case. Many players have come up from the lowest of circumstances in order to even get to the league, and in doing so, they have inspired fans across the world who either dream of getting into the NBA or are finding themselves in the same rough spots and need that assurance they'll come out of them. Here are the stories of ten inspiring NBA stars who have fought through significant hardships and won.

Allen Iverson

Allen Iverson came from a harsh upbringing, his mother had him when she was just fifteen, and his father wasn't around to help raise him. His father figure was arrested right in front of him for dealing drugs, and he flunked the eighth grade due to racking up more than a few absences. The worst of it all came in 1993 when he was involved in a fight in a bowling alley between his friends and a group of white kids around his age at the age of seventeen. Iverson was arrested, and in a racially-biased trial, he was sentenced to fifteen years in jail. However, he was released less than a year later due to leniency and lack of evidence. The experience reinforced his never-back-down attitude, which was reflected in how he played basketball. His skills resulted in him being picked first in the 1996 NBA Draft, and eventually, he would go down as one of the greatest point guards the league has ever seen.

Lebron James

The story of Lebron James proves your circumstances don't have to dictate who you are. He was born to a single mother who was only sixteen, and they lived in Akron, Ohio, a notoriously poor section of Cleveland. In order to give her son a better life, his mother Gloria allowed him to move in with a local youth football coach named Frank Waller. Frank was the one who actually introduced Lebron to basketball, which made all the difference. In time, Lebron excelled at the sport and became a high-school sensation, and he was drafted straight out of high school as the first pick in the 2003 NBA draft. Now he's a multi-time NBA champion, lives in a mansion in Los Angeles, and has opened up his own elementary school in Akron that serves at-risk children.

Muggsy Bogues

Height is an important tangible in the NBA; it's a much-needed advantage to get shots over your defenders and grab the ball for a block or rebound. The average height of an NBA player is 6'6." Muggsy Bogues is 5'3." He came into the league at a major disadvantage. 6'3" was already considered short for NBA standards. And yet he didn't let his physical limitations deter him, and his stature meant he could quickly lose his defenders and work around the big men in the post for a basket. He was a valued member of any team he was on; he started for two-thirds of his games in his fourteen-year career. Other players that have excelled at their game despite their shorter stature include Nate Robinson (5'9"), Wataru Misaka (5'7"), Spud Webb (5'6"), and Earl Boykins (5'5"). Muggsy also starred in the movie *Space Jam*.

Trevor Ariza

Losing a loved one is always challenging, and the grief that comes from it can easily take a person over. In 1996, Trevor Ariza and his mother were watching his stepfather play basketball when he got the news that his brother Tajh fell thirty stories out a hotel window to his death. He felt intense grief, but he refused to let the trauma break him. Trevor used basketball as a way to cope, and in doing so, Trevor became a disciplined and talented player. He would be a star in UCLA and would, later on, have a great career in the NBA that included winning a championship with the Lakers. He named his first son after his brother. An honorable mention goes to Isaiah Thomas. During the 2017 playoffs, his sister Chyna died in a car accident. The very next day, Isaiah suited up and led the Celtics in their game against the Bulls. Despite being full of emotions and grief, he recorded thirty-three points, six assists, and five rebounds. Maybe Trevor needed to play this game in order to keep the heartache from overtaking him, or perhaps he knew his team needed him in this series. Though the Celtics ended up losing the game, Isaiah earned massive respect from NBA fans everywhere, and he got the chance to honor his sister, and so did the thousands of people in attendance that day.

Michael Jordan

When you follow your dreams, there will always be walls in the way keeping you from going forward. How you handle them will say a lot about your motivation and your character. Michael Jordan was infamously cut from his basketball team as a sophomore in high school, they posted the roster for the varsity team, and when Michael didn't see his name on it, he was angry. But he turned that anger into determination and continued to work on his game. Eventually, he would become one of the greatest basketball players of all time. How different would the NBA look if Michael Jordan gave up after that one failure?

Chuck Cooper, Nat Clifton, and Earl Lloyd

Adversity comes in many forms. The NBA wasn't always as diverse as it is today. It was an all-white league when it first started, and black people weren't even considered for roster spots. This was during a time when racism was rampant and incredibly public. Black people were deemed to be inferior and weren't given the same opportunities as their white counterparts. These three black men make the list together because they were the first ones to break the color barrier in the NBA. Chuck Cooper was the first black player to be drafted onto a team (the Celtics), Nat Clifton was the first to sign a contract, and Earl Lloyd was the first black man actually to play a game in the NBA. Each man defied society's prejudices and took a necessary step in paving the way for more black people to join the league.

Magic Johnson

Magic's life is one in which he's consistently had to overcome the odds. He was diagnosed with dyslexia and ADD as a kid, making reading and overall learning very difficult. Through hard work, a determined Magic overcame both these things and learned how to read. Later in life, when he was one of the hottest stars in the NBA, tragedy struck when he was diagnosed with HIV in 1991. Not a lot was known about the disease during this time, so the diagnosis forced him to retire from the NBA immediately. His diagnosis brought so much more awareness to the disease, and scientists did more research to understand better how to identify and fight HIV. Magic was hailed as a hero, and despite his retirement, he was voted into the 1992 All-Star Game and played in the Olympics that same year. His living a fulfilled life despite the disease inspired everyone, but most of all, other HIV-positive people.

Isiah Thomas

This is a tale of one of the greatest moments in the NBA playoffs and of a leader stepping up when his team needed him the most. It's game six of the 1988 NBA Finals, the Pistons are up against the Lakers 3-2, and one more win will seal the championship for them. Point guard Isiah Thomas has scored fourteen points in the third quarter, and then things take a turn for the worst when he rolls his ankle. He leaves the court, and with the Pistons now lacking their leader, the Lakers take advantage and go up by eight points. In a brave show of strength, Thomas hobbles back onto the court with the third quarter winding down and checks himself back in. He's working with one good leg, yet he plays like that doesn't even matter, knocking down eleven more points to give the Pistons the lead in the fourth quarter. The amount of pain he was in must have been astounding, but Thomas knew his team needed him, and that's all that mattered.

Chris Andersen

You can always pull yourself back up again no matter how far you fall. In the early 2000s, Chris Andersen joined the league and became a reliable backup center. That all changed in January 2006, when he was suspended from the NBA for violating their substance abuse policy. He would not be allowed back in the NBA for two years. During that time, he stayed busy by going into rehab, working out, and wanting to stay involved with the sport he coached on a boys' basketball team in Denver. He was reinstated in January 2008 and worked his way back into becoming the reliable player he knew he could be. His best days were with the 2012-2013 Miami Heat, where he contributed to their inevitable championship win.

Jimmy Butler

We end the chapter by looking at one man who never gave up on himself no matter how much life threw at him. Jimmy Butler was born in 1989 in Tomball, Texas; his father left shortly after his birth and left his mother to take care of him alone. He leaned on sports to keep him occupied and out of trouble, but trouble came for him anyway. At the age of thirteen, his mother kicked him out of the house and effectively rendered him homeless. Jimmy bounced around from couch to couch, never really staying in one place for too long, and even spent some nights in the gym. Then during his junior year, a friend showed great kindness to him by allowing him to stay with his family until he could get on his feet again. During this time, Jimmy continued to improve as a basketball player and caught the eye of a Marquette scout who wanted him to join their program. He accepted, but the coach was so tough on him that he wanted to quit altogether. But Jimmy Butler had come too far to quit now, and he inevitably blossomed into the player he always knew he could be. Finally, his dream to make a living out of playing basketball came true when the Chicago Bulls drafted him as the thirtieth pick in the 2011 NBA Draft. The kid from Texas with a dream went from being homeless to finding a home in the NBA.

Chapter 7: Greatest Underdog Wins

The underdog story is one that will never get old, especially when it comes to sports. Everyone loves to watch the overlooked, out-of-nowhere character manage to defy the odds and accomplish a feat that most thought impossible. Perhaps these stories are so popular because it's easy for people to relate to the underdogs. Everyone's been in a situation where they've been up against incredible pressure, and sometimes... well, sometimes things don't go our way. But when we look to the underdogs, it's like giving ourselves a second chance. So when they win, it's elating and invigorating; you feel inspired and hopeful that you can beat the odds one day. The NBA is full of great underdog victories, ones where it seems like victory is no longer an option for a team, and suddenly they come back to win it all. Here are eight moments in the NBA when teams have taken on the underdog role and come back from the greatest of challenges.

"We Believe"

Being the eighth seed in the playoffs doesn't necessarily mean you're the easiest team to beat on the road to the championship; it just means you have the most challenging road getting there. The 2006-2007 Golden State Warriors were in this position, coming into the playoffs as the eighth seed against a hungry Dallas Mavericks team looking to avenge their loss in the Finals the previous season. This Warriors team almost didn't make the playoffs at all. They started the season only winning nineteen of their first forty games. With the help of a mid-season, eight-person trade that saw them acquiring key players Al Harrington and Stephen Jackson, the Warriors finally found some footing and started stringing some wins together. Now coach Don Nelson had a playoff-worthy team consisting of the players mentioned above and emerging power forward Matt Barnes, talented shooting guard Jason Richardson, and fan-favorite Baron Davis. Fans were delighted, backing up their team's improving performance, and the team was subsequently dubbed the "We Believe" Warriors. With a team full of great players but no clear star, the team was now faced with the task of beating a sixty-win Mavericks team… *and they did*. In six games, inside the Oracle Arena and amidst a sea of fans wearing t-shirts adorned with the words "We Believe," the Warriors overcame the odds and advanced to the second round of the playoffs. And even though they would inevitably lose in that round to the Jazz, no one will ever forget their performance that made everyone believe for at least a moment. Eight seasons later, the Warriors would give them a reason to believe again.

Game Seven Heroics

It's hard to believe that the legendary Lakers three-peat was twelve minutes away from never happening. It's game seven of the 2000 Western Conference Finals between the Lakers and Blazers, who have just engineered an amazing comeback after being down 3-1 in the series. Not only have they pushed the best of the West to seven games, but they've also got them on the ropes coming into the fourth quarter. The Lakers are down by fifteen, the clock is winding down, and the Blazers' stellar defense has essentially neutralized their best weapon in Shaquille O' Neal. Things were looking bleak in the Staples Center, and then with ten minutes left in the game, the Lakers finally woke up. The comeback begins with Brian Shaw knocking down a few much-needed threes, which succeeded in helping Diesel rev up his engine and reminding the Portland defense who he is. With two minutes left, Shaq threw up a hook shot that found the bottom of the net and gave the Lakers the lead. What had the Blazers been doing this whole time? Missing. A lot. Instead of closing this game out, the Blazers missed twelve shots in a row and gave the Lakers some room to breathe. A minute later, Kobe and Shaq completed one of the most iconic plays in playoff history. Kobe has the ball and sizes up elite veteran Scottie Pippen before losing him with a wicked crossover. He drives to the hoop with the basket insight and suddenly lobs the ball up high to a waiting Shaq, who completes the alley-oop pass with an emphatic dunk roaring the entire arena. A few short seconds later, the game is over. The Lakers completed one of the greatest fourth-quarter comebacks in NBA history. They inevitably go on to win the championship for the first of three consecutive times.

13 in 33

The game isn't over until the final buzzer rings, and Tracy McGrady made sure everyone knew that in December 2004. It's late in the game for a regular-season encounter between the Rockets and Spurs. How late? There are about forty seconds left in the fourth quarter. The Spurs are up 76-68, and that's unlikely to change unless a miracle happens. Enter Tracy McGrady, the Rockets star who's decided he wants to make that miracle happen. Burning seven seconds off the clock, McGrady books it down the court, gets a screen and splashes in a three. Now with thirty-five seconds left, the Rockets quickly foul, and the Spurs make both of their free throws. Thirty-one seconds on the clock and the scenario replays itself, McGrady has the ball and gets a screen, but he makes sure to draw the foul as he makes his three in order to get the opportunity for a four-point play. McGrady makes his free throw, the Rockets are only down by three, and there are twenty-four seconds left in the game. The Spurs make two more free throws, but now Tracy McGrady's feeling it. After an inbound pass that almost ends in a backcourt violation, he finds his sweet spot and banks in another three with eleven captivating seconds left. The crowd that has stuck around knows they're about to witness something great, and they cheer their star on. After a tense timeout, the Spurs inbound the ball from their side of the court, burn four more seconds, and then the unthinkable happens: they turn the ball over. Quickly, the Rockets get the ball into McGrady's hands. The clock reaches four seconds as he steps up to the arc. He lets the ball fly and finds the bottom of the net for the fourth time. The crowd roars, and so does McGrady as he punches the air with the adrenaline pumping. Two seconds, one defensive play, and a missed shot later, the Rockets completed their miraculous comeback thanks to Tracy McGrady's thirteen points in thirty-three seconds.

The Biggest Comeback

Sometimes, a comeback lasts a little longer than thirty-three seconds. It's November 1996, and their own fans have just booed the Jazz as they walk into the locker room for halftime. Why have they turned against their team? Well, because the scoreboard reads 70-36, and their team is on the wrong side of that score. Their opponents that night, the Denver Nuggets, have been embarrassing them all game, and in the locker room, coach Jerry Sloan lets them know it. Something has to change, and as both teams walk out for the second half, that change is in the air. The comeback began with nine minutes left in the third quarter, and the score was 74-41. The Jazz finally started finding the bottom of the net, stars John Stockton and Karl Malone remembered that they were John Stockton and Karl Malone, and Jeff Hornacek started scoring buckets in a big way.

After a phenomenal scoring run, the third quarter ended with a score of 85-72. The Nuggets were still winning, but things didn't look as bleak. In the fourth quarter, the Jazz continued their offensive assault and lock-down defense, going on a 19-6 run to *finally* tie up the game. The Nuggets found some offense again and kept the game interesting, matching the Jazz shot for shot until there was just a minute left. A three from Jeff Hornacek solidified the lead for the Jazz, along with a turnover by the Nuggets that they converted with a dunk. With six seconds left in the game, John Stockton hit two free throws to make the game truly out of reach, and the Jazz completed the most incredible comeback in NBA regular-season history, winning the game with a score of 107-103. The Nuggets would get their revenge in the 2020 playoffs, coming back from a 3-1 deficit to take the series.

The Undeniables

This section is dedicated not to the teams but to the players who have achieved great comebacks of their own. Whether they came back from injuries, hardships, or even retirement, their stories can be just as inspiring and wonderful to relive. In 2014, during a Team USA scrimmage, Paul George suffered a gruesome leg injury that took him out for the season. During this time, he was a legitimate All-Star hoping to take the Pacers all the way to an NBA championship. Many wondered if Paul would ever have that same impact on the court ever again. Thankfully, Paul George made a full recovery and brought his career back on track. As of now, he's the star player for the Los Angeles Clippers. In 1977, Celtics player Dave Cowens lost all passion for the game and left after the season was over. He worked as a cab driver for a little bit before the passion returned to him, and he rejoined the team. That next season, he set team records for points, assists, rebounds, steals, and blocks that helped take the Celtics to the playoffs. Willis Reed was coming into the 1970 NBA Finals with a torn muscle in his thigh, the kind of injury definitely not worth aggravating. It sidelined him for game six, but knowing that the Knicks needed him, he decided to suit up for game seven. As Willis limped out of the tunnel in Madison Square Garden, the fans went wild, especially when he made his first two shots of the game. He sat out the rest of the game, but he had given his team all the motivation they needed to close out the series and bring the championship to the Knicks. Michael Jordan first retired due to burnout and wanting to live up to his late father's wishes to play professional baseball. After a less-than-stellar run in the minor leagues and some persuasion from his Chicago team and fans, Michael Jordan uttered two words: "I'm back." He would make his triumphant return to the Chicago Bulls in 1995 and would lead them to a second three-peat with the NBA championship. While these are all great comebacks from great players, they don't necessarily fit the image of an underdog. There is one player that fits the underdog image, and to tell his story, we have to travel back to 2012 when the league was swept up in a little something called…

Linsanity

Jeremy Lin's NBA career mirrored a lot of hopeful athletes who withered from lack of opportunities in the league. The Asian-American point guard was coming off a stellar few years playing for Harvard and decided to enter the 2010 NBA Draft. Lin watched as other college stars like John Wall, Demarcus Cousins, and Paul George got their names called, hoping as the round continued that his name would be called as the round continued. The first round passed by, and soon so did the second, without Lin's name ever being called. Teams were wary of picking him due to scout reports saying that he has a weak jumper, couldn't create his own shot, and didn't have the strength needed to be a good defender. But going undrafted wasn't the end for him; he wouldn't let it be. The Dallas Mavericks picked him up to train with them and play for them in the Summer League. Jeremy Lin impressed everyone in those games, putting up nearly ten points and three rebounds per game, and by the end of it, he had received several contract offers. He ended up signing a deal with the Warriors, which made him the first Taiwanese-American to ever play in the NBA. Though he'd finally gotten his ticket into the league, the hardships wouldn't end there. The Warriors already had two point guards, which meant Lin was a very distant third option. On the rare occasion he'd get minutes, they'd usually be late in the game when victory was either inevitable or far out of reach, but he made the most out of his time regardless. He would flip-flop between being on the Warriors bench and playing for their D-League affiliate until December 2011, when they waived him. Fortunately, he would be picked up by the Rockets just three days later. Unfortunately, the Rockets also waived him before the season started. Lin's roller coaster of a career continued as the Knicks claimed him for the season (Great!) as their fourth-option point guard (Not great!). Lin couldn't be farther on the bench if he tried, but even so, he continued to work on himself and his game. He built up muscle, worked on his shooting form, improved his footwork, and put in insane work during practices; he'd come too far to back down now. Despite continuing to ride the bench, Lin continued to bet on himself, and that gamble finally paid off on February 4, 2012. The three-point guards before him had failed to run the offense that coach Mike D'Antoni put together, and he'd finally run out of options. The Knicks were facing off against the Nets and their All-Star point guard Deron Williams; if Lin didn't perform well, he would probably kiss his contract and maybe even his career goodbye. But that didn't happen. In his first real chance to prove himself in a non-D-League game, Jeremy Lin put up twenty-five points, five rebounds, and seven assists to a much-needed Knicks victory. He was put in as their starting point guard the next game and dropped twenty-eight points to notch another win for the Knicks. D'Antoni kept him in the starting lineup, and the team won seven straight games. Linsanity was here. Highlights of that winning streak include crossing up John Wall, the number one pick of his draft class, dropping thirty-eight points against former NBA champions the Los Angeles Lakers and the infamous game-winner in Toronto.

At the peak of Linsanity, in front of the Toronto crowd, Jeremy Lin had the ball with fifteen seconds left during a tied game. He waved off screens and beckoned his defender to step back as he stood near half-court. Lin advanced slowly with the ball as the fans rose to their feet, waiting to see greatness as the clock winded down. With two seconds left, he pulled up from just behind the three-point line fearlessly and watched the ball go in. The fans went wild as he confidently made his way back to his team. Linsanity was short-lived, and its aftermath was messy. Still, for that brief moment in time, NBA fans were treated to one of the greatest stories in league history: the undrafted, overlooked player given an opportunity on the big stage and making the most of it. It was inspiring, especially to Asian-American fans who finally had a hero to look up to in sports media that looked like them.

The Dark Horse

We went into a little bit of detail on this while talking about Dirk Nowitzki's career, but the Mavericks' championship run deserves a deeper look. 2011 going into the playoffs, a few teams were predicted to win the championship. You had, of course, the Lakers who were the defending champions and looking for another three-peat, the Heat and their newly assembled Big Three, the Bulls with their young MVP Derrick Rose, the "Grit and Grind" Grizzlies, and the always-contending Spurs. A team that wasn't being talked up: the Dallas Mavericks. Despite being the third seed in the West, the Mavericks weren't being picked to make it all the way to the Finals. Yet they were still aiming to impress as a dark horse candidate. The Mavericks exemplified what "team effort" truly meant throughout the playoffs. Though Dirk Nowitzki was their clear leader, their cast of role players shared offensive and defensive efforts, including veteran Jason Kidd, offensive big man Tyson Chandler, sharpshooter Jason Terry, and defensive threat Shawn Marion. They first proved that they shouldn't be counted out when they beat Brandon Roy and the Blazers in six games. They had the defending champions to look forward to in the next round, who was sure to make them work for their wins. And then… they swept them. The Mavericks won four straight games against the Lakers and punched their ticket to the Western Conference Finals. Could they actually do this? They next matched up with the younger and faster Oklahoma City Thunder, with rising stars Kevin Durant, Russel Westbrook, and James Harden in their arsenal. Surely, this would be where their underdog story ended. Surely a team full of aging veterans couldn't take down the team full of future All-Stars. No, the Mavericks wouldn't be denied, and they beat the Thunder in five games. Finally, they had to contend with the villains of the East, the superteam, the Miami Heat. Everyone on the Mavericks stepped up in a big way, especially Dirk, who wanted to shake off the criticism of being too soft and an incapable leader. The Mavericks held Lebron to only eighteen points per game, and Dirk made the rest of the opposing team look like fools as he made basket after basket. One crucial highlight occurred in a series-altering game two; the game was tied up with fifteen seconds left, and the Mavericks had the ball. Jason Kidd passed it to Dirk, who took the fate of the game into his own hands. He lost his defender with a spin move and drove into the lane to lay the ball up, give the Mavericks the win, and tie the series at 1-1. Four games later, the dark horse won the race, the Mavericks hoisted the NBA championship up high and became one of the most unlikely teams ever to do so.

Cleveland, This is For You

It's 2016, the NBA Finals are drawing to a close in a nail-biting game seven, and an unfulfilled promise lingers in the Oracle Arena. It's difficult to imagine the number one team in the East as an underdog, but that's what the Cleveland Cavaliers find themselves as. After a fruitless first run with the team and a few years down in South Beach, Lebron James made his return to the Cavaliers with a promise that he would bring the championship home to a city that hadn't won a major league championship in more than fifty years. In his first year back with the team, they managed to make it back to the Finals. Still, critical injuries to Kevin Love and Kyrie Irving saw the Golden State Warriors holding the championship up high instead of the Cavaliers. This time, this year, they would be ready. They had to be. They had the best record in the East at the end of the 2015-2016 season and would enter the playoffs as the first seed. They made quick work of the Pistons in the first round and the Hawks in the second. The Toronto Raptors were the one team left in their path back to the Finals. Much like the Cavaliers, the Raptors were a team that had a healthy balance of stars and role players. But they didn't have Lebron James. After splitting the first four games, the Cavaliers blew them out in games five and six. Once again, the Cavaliers were in the NBA Finals. Once again, their opponents were the Warriors, a team that had just gone 73-9 in the regular season. The Warriors set the pace by blowing out the Cavaliers in the first two games, though Lebron and company returned the favor in game three. The next game was crucial for the Cavaliers, and even though Lebron and Kyrie piled on the points, Steph Curry and Klay Thompson one-upped them, and the Warriors snatched the victory. The Warriors were now up 3-1, and the Cavaliers needed to win every game from here on out if they wanted to survive. In-game five, both Lebron and Kyrie went off to score forty-one points each and take the victory for the team. Hope stayed alive. In-game six, Lebron put up forty-one again, and with a balanced attack by a rejuvenated team, the Cavaliers took game six as well.

Everything came down to this—game seven. The game remained close throughout the first three quarters through both sides' superb defense and shot selection. The fourth quarter saw much of the same. They traded baskets as much as they traded misses; both sides stared each other down, waiting for the other one to blink. And then, with the score perpetually tied 89-89, the Warriors finally did. With two minutes left, Andre Iguodala rebounded a missed layup by Kyrie and brought the ball up on the fast break. With a clear shot to the basket, he went for a layup of his own, and then from out of nowhere, he was blocked from behind by Lebron James. One possession later, Kyrie would redeem himself by hitting a clutch three, inevitably signaling the end to one of the most exciting Finals series of all time. Finally fulfilling his promise, Lebron lets his emotions go during a postgame interview, exclaiming cathartically, "Cleveland! This is for you!"

Conclusion

As you dribble your ball across the driveway, the same game plays out in your mind. With the same crowd, the same ten seconds on the clock, the same defender waiting to snatch victory literally out of your hands. But this time, you decide not to go for the step-back jumper. Maybe you'll go with the crossover-like A.I., and perhaps you'll back your defender down a little bit before going for Dirk's fadeaway; maybe you'll drive into the paint and go for Kareem's skyhook. You have so many options, and you know all about the greats, you know basketball on a whole different level, a fundamentally incredible level.

The NBA has been around for nearly a century, and now you, wonderful reader, have the knowledge of almost a century's worth of history. As long as there's basketball to be played, the NBA will always be around, which means it will be more important that this knowledge remains available as the years go by. Forgetting all of this history would be tragic, but thankfully that won't happen with readers like you preserving this information and sharing it with other eager basketball fans. In this book, you not only learned how the NBA formed but also how basketball itself came to be. You saw the changes made to the game and its evolution into what we see on T.V. today. You found out more about the five primary positions on a basketball team and their responsibilities and also took a look at some of the greatest players of all time to play at each of these positions. You strategized with ten of the greatest coaches in the game. You discovered many fun facts and forgotten bits of NBA history. And you read the tales of some of the most inspiring players and underdog teams that rose up from the worst of circumstances and the greatest of odds.

I hope this book has helped you to appreciate the sport of basketball and the NBA much more. There are so many stories that have yet to be told in the league and so much history on the hardwood that deserves to be remembered. Use your newfound knowledge to impress your friends and family and show them that there's more to the game than they see on the court. And when they want to learn more about what makes this game so unique, you'll know exactly which book to recommend.

References

Bailey, A. (2020, July 25). Ranking the 50 Best NBA Teams of All Time. *Bleacher Report*. https://bleacherreport.com/articles/2901057-ranking-the-50-best-nba-teams-of-all-time

Basketball Positions: Key Roles and Responsibilities (explained). (2018, February 26). Basketball for Coaches. https://www.basketballforcoaches.com/basketball-positions/

Bazzocchi, D. (2021, July 8). *Fun Facts About The NBA - OwnersBox*. OwnersBox Blog. https://blog.ownersbox.com/uncategorized/fun-facts-about-the-nba/

Biography.com Editors. (2015, June 18). *James Naismith*. Biography; A&E Television Networks. https://www.biography.com/scholar/james-a-naismith

Bois, J. (2013, August 27). 13 points, 33 seconds: *The night Tracy McGrady was a basketball god*. SBNation.com. https://www.sbnation.com/2013/8/27/4661546/tracy-mcgrady-13-points-33-seconds

Chicago Bulls History. (n.d.). Chicago Bulls. https://www.nba.com/bulls/history/players/phil-jackson

Chin, D. (2022, February 4). *The Legacy of Linsanity, 10 Years Later*. The Ringer; The Ringer. https://www.theringer.com/nba/2022/2/4/22916972/jeremy-lin-linsanity-knicks-asian-american-representation-10th-anniversary

Conway, T. (2014, April 28). *Dr. Jack Ramsay, Former NBA Coach and Hall of Famer, Passes Away at Age 89.* Bleacher Report; Bleacher Report. https://bleacherreport.com/articles/2043967-dr-jack-ramsay-former-nba-coach-and-hall-of-famer-passes-away-at-age-89

D'Amico, M. (n.d.). *A Look at the Legends: Red Auerbach.* Boston Celtics. https://www.nba.com/celtics/history/legends/red-auerbach

Dorsey, J. (2011, November 1). *The 50 Most Inspirational Figures in NBA History.* Bleacher Report. https://bleacherreport.com/articles/919860-50-most-inspirational-figures-in-nba-history

Fromal, A. (2011, October 28). *10 Greatest Comeback Stories in NBA History.* Bleacher Report. https://bleacherreport.com/articles/914607-10-greatest-comeback-stories-in-nba-history

Gregg Popovich. (n.d.). Basketball-Reference.com. https://www.basketball-reference.com/coaches/popovgr99c.html

History. (n.d.). NBA Careers. https://careers.nba.com/history/#:~:text=The%20NBA%20is%20a%2070

History of basketball. (2021, July 16). Wikipedia. https://en.wikipedia.org/wiki/History_of_basketball#cite_note-Republican-2

Jazz 107, Nuggets 103. (1996, November 28). AP NEWS. https://apnews.com/article/9b8eaaddf9ee902ffd9433d342f02150

Keefe, M. (2012, April 7). *NBA: Gregg Popovich and the Best System Coaches.* Bleacher Report. https://bleacherreport.com/articles/1136191-greg-popovich-and-the-best-system-coaches

Kidadl Team. (2021, August 29). *110+ NBA Trivia Questions (And Answers): Can You Get A Slamdunk?* Kidadl.com. https://kidadl.com/articles/nba-trivia-questions-and-answers-can-you-get-a-slamdunk

Larry Brown (basketball). (2022, February 22). Wikipedia. https://en.wikipedia.org/wiki/Larry_Brown_(basketball)#Early_life_and_early_basketball_accomplishments

List of NBA regular-season records. (2022, January 3). Wikipedia. https://en.wikipedia.org/wiki/List_of_NBA_regular_season_records#:~:text=The%20longest%20NBA%20game%20occurred

Longtime Jazz coach Jerry Sloan dies at age 78. (2020, May 22). ESPN.com. https://www.espn.com/nba/story/_/id/29209339/long-jazz-coach-jerry-sloan-dies-age-78

Martin, G. (2020, June 16). *Top 5 Best Players Of All-Time At Each Position.* Fadeaway World. https://fadeawayworld.net/nba/top-5-best-players-of-all-time-at-each-position

NBA.com Staff. (2021a, September 13). *Legends profile: David Robinson.* National Basketball Association. https://www.nba.com/news/history-nba-legend-david-robinson

NBA.com Staff. (2021b, September 13). *Legends profile: Lenny Wilkens.* Www.nba.com. https://www.nba.com/news/history-nba-legend-lenny-wilkens

NBA.com Staff. (2021c, September 14). *Top Moments: Isiah Thomas heroically hobbles to record a 25-point quarter in the Finals.* Www.nba.com. https://www.nba.com/news/history-top-moments-isiah-thomas-25-points

Neumann, T. (2021, April 1). *The 101 greatest nicknames in NBA history.* The Rookie Wire. https://therookiewire.usatoday.com/lists/greatest-nicknames-in-nba-history/

Oswell, K. (2020, May 11). *10 Basketball Facts You Didn't Know*. Red Bull. https://www.redbull.com/us-en/basketball-facts

Ramirez, J. (2017, July 24). *John Kundla: Legacy of the Lakers' First Coach*. Los Angeles Lakers. https://www.nba.com/lakers/news/170724-john-kundla

Ramirez, J. (2020, March 30). *Lakers History: The 15-Point, 4th-Quarter Comeback in Game 7*. Los Angeles Lakers. https://www.nba.com/lakers/news/180829-lakers-day-shaq-kobe-lead-15-point-game-7-comeback

Red Auerbach. (2022, February 23). Wikipedia. https://en.wikipedia.org/wiki/Red_Auerbach#General_manager_(1966%E2%80%9384)

See, S. (2020, July 4). *Ranking The 10 Greatest NBA Teams Of All Time*. ClutchPoints. https://clutchpoints.com/ranking-the-10-greatest-nba-teams-of-all-time/

See, S. (2021, December 1). *24 Strangest Facts About the NBA*. ClutchPoints. https://clutchpoints.com/strange-nba-facts-ranked-from-24-to-1/

Sevilleja, T. (2021, June 15). *NBA Playoffs: Ranking the 5 Greatest Underdog Runs This Century*. ClutchPoints. https://clutchpoints.com/nba-playoffs-ranking-the-5-greatest-underdog-runs-this-century/

Shoals, B. (n.d.). *Pat Riley | Biography & Facts | Britannica*. Www.britannica.com. https://www.britannica.com/biography/Pat-Riley

Steve Nash. (n.d.). Basketball Wiki. https://basketball.fandom.com/wiki/Steve_Nash

Warond, A. (2017, May 30). *The Most Inspiring NBA Story Ever: From Homeless To All-Star*. Fadeaway World. https://

fadeawayworld.com/more-than-points/the-most-inspiring-nba-story-ever-from-homeless-to-all-star

Wikipedia Contributors. (2019a, February 17). *National Basketball Association*. Wikipedia; Wikimedia Foundation. https://en.wikipedia.org/wiki/National_Basketball_Association

Wikipedia Contributors. (2019b, October 2). *National Basketball League (United States)*. Wikipedia; Wikimedia Foundation. https://en.wikipedia.org/wiki/National_Basketball_League_(United_States)

Wikipedia Contributors. (2019c, November 8). *NBA Global Games*. Wikipedia; Wikimedia Foundation. https://en.wikipedia.org/wiki/NBA_Global_Games

Wikipedia Contributors. (2019d, November 14). *Phil Jackson*. Wikipedia; Wikimedia Foundation. https://en.wikipedia.org/wiki/Phil_Jackson

Wikipedia Contributors. (2019e, November 29). *Don Nelson*. Wikipedia; Wikimedia Foundation. https://en.wikipedia.org/wiki/Don_Nelson

Ziller, T. (2019, November 7). *NBA head coaching jobs are increasingly stable*. SBNation.com. https://www.sbnation.com/nba/2019/11/7/20951269/nba-head-coaching-jobs-turnover-statistics

www.ingramcontent.com/pod-product-compliance
Lightning Source LLC
Chambersburg PA
CBHW030305100526
44590CB00012B/529